# Here's what reviewers

## Wild River Guide to Dism~

### including waterways of northeastern North Carolina

"I am genuinely interested in the history of these waterways and the people and places that laid the foundations of the early development of our country. The area covered by this guide is steeped in this history. The guide also offers a view of the plants and animals that populate these special places. The authors have gone to great lengths to combine all of these subjects into a very usable and interesting guide. I will definitely be using it to visit those areas that I have missed."

— George Ramsey
Southeast Virginia Director
Virginia Canals and Navigations Society

"The thorough details and descriptions make the *Wild River Guide to Dismal Swamp Water Trails* essential for the serious or casual paddler, and its rich historical and ecological content make it an excellent guide for the 'armchair' paddler as well."

— W. Michael Lane
Izaak Walton League of America
Suffolk-Nansemond Chapter (VA)

"The detailed maps, historic (and prehistoric) connections, geological and biological features described in each section entices the reader to not only read further but desire to experience the waterways firsthand."

— Byron Carmean
Naturalist and Outdoor Educator

"The book is gorgeous. It will be attractive to kayak and canoe campers, the long distance travelers, as well as the day-trippers."

— William H. Spaur
Captain, Medical Corps, USN, Retired

"It's great! The maps, history, natural history and photos make this a useful guide for paddlers and others interested in our cultural and natural history."

— Bill Petree
Parks Coordinator, City of Chesapeake

# Also by Lillie Gilbert and Vickie Shufer

*Wild River Guide to the North Landing River
and its tributaries*

ISBN: 0-938423-06-1

# Wild River Guide to Dismal Swamp Water Trails

### including waterways
### of northeastern North Carolina

*Number 2 in a Series of Guidebooks*
*for Paddlers, Naturalists and Historians*

by Lillie Gilbert and Vickie Shufer

**Virginia Beach, Virginia**

Published by:
**ECO IMAGES**
P.O. Box 61413
Virginia Beach, Virginia 23466-1413
Email: wildfood@infionline.net
URL: http://wildfood.home.infionline.net

Cover photo by Pati Terry

ISBN: 0-938423-11-8

Copies of this book available from:
**Wild River Outfitters, Inc.**
3636 Virginia Beach Blvd. #108
Virginia Beach, VA 23452
Phone: 757.431.8566
Fax: 757.340.1098
Email: mail@wildriveroutfitters.com
URL: www.wildriveroutfitters.com

Printed in the United States of America

First Printing

*Dedicated to the memory of Pat Cuffee:*
*one who walked softly*
*and lived with great spirit and generosity.*
*A member of the Great Dismal Swamp Coalition,*
*Pat will be remembered as a*
*naturalist, photographer, long-time friend and volunteer*
*of the Great Dismal Swamp.*

# Table of Contents

# River Map Contents

# Foreword

In 1967 I arrived in what was then known as the Tidewater area to begin my duties as an Assistant Professor at Old Dominion College. On the road map I used to plan our trip to Norfolk, I noticed a place called "The Great Dismal Swamp." Having spent time exploring the remnants of the Black Swamp of Ohio and many northern swamps in Wisconsin, I was intrigued. The question was how did one get into the Great Dismal? I soon found that there was no readily available answer to this question especially for a recent "come here" who knew almost no one.

In my case it began by studying many maps and gradually making local contacts. Eventually I found that a trip back to my native New Jersey and the headquarters of the Union Camp Corporation was the way to unlock the gates to the many Dismal Swamp roads. This was necessary as at that time the swamp was completely under private ownership.

It was about three years after my arrival, while visiting the Colonial Williamsburg Visitor Center, that I found the excellent, just published, "The Dismal Swamp Canal" by Alexander Crosby Brown (1970). Even though I now realized that the Feeder Ditch was another gate to the Dismal, at that time there were few convenient places to put in a small boat or canoe as nearby public accesses were virtually nonexistent. Eventually with the help of several others we managed to lower a canoe down the very steep bank near the entrance to the Feeder Ditch. We then proceeded to the Corps of Engineers' spillway and thus to the lake. Over the years I discovered the joys of exploring the swamp and its jewel, Lake Drummond via its various ditches. The Northwest River and Back Bay were also explored as my knowledge expanded.

Now the native and the "come here" no longer have to go through such an arduous process. With the publication of this marvelous resource, Lillie Gilbert and Vickie Shufer have made it possible for the small boater and paddle enthusiast to plan out a brief day's excursion or a major expedition in our region. Not only does one now know where to put in, but also what to look for historically and biologically and how far it is to get to where one wishes to be. They also tell us where to find additional information. Laid out in a clear, delightfully easy to read format are maps, synopses of the extensive background literature and references which include the results of the last thirty years of scholarly research that has bundled together the widely scattered historical studies as well as the latest historical and scientific research.

On behalf of all those who will derive so much from your efforts, thank you Lillie and Vickie. I wish all the users of this book years of pleasure exploring the wonders of our Dismal Swamp waterways.

Dr. Gerald F. Levy, Ph.D.
Professor Emeritus
Department of Biological Sciences
Old Dominion University

*Photo by Pat Cuffee*

# Acknowledgements

Many people were involved in the making of this book and we thank you so very much. For permission to use their research books, photographs or artwork, we are grateful to "Spike" Knuth, Melinda and Reese Lukei, Rhonda Morris, Edgar Brown, Pat Cuffee, Jay Wadsworth, Anne Henry, Elizabeth Baum Hanbury, George Ramsey, Lauren Gansemer and REB Stewart. Thanks to Gerald Levy for sharing his knowledge of the Dismal Swamp and for the weekends spent exploring and working on projects in the swamp. Thanks to Jerry Hoddinott of the Chesapeake Public Utilities for providing information pertinent to the Northwest River Water Treatment Plant. Travis Morris shared memories of Currituck County. Jim Overman, Director of Parks and Recreation, Elizabeth City, was helpful concerning access points in the city. Lynette Bruggeman, Director of Tourism, City of Suffolk, enthusiastically gave support and shared information concerning Suffolk. John Gillikin and Patti Gilbert took a special interest in our tide mill questions and led us to several excellent websites. Penny Leary-Smith, Director of the Dismal Swamp Visitor Center, filled in some gaps in data and pored over maps with us to share her local knowledge. Special thanks to Ned Williams for the use of his cabin and to the Teague family for their hospitality and use of their guest cottage during some of our scouting trips.

Others with whom we spoke are numerous and we apologize if we have left anyone out, but we would like to recognize the contributions of Mary Keith Garrett, Pat Gammon, Jim and Katherine Wassing, Tom Campbell, Fred Fearing, Bill Petree, Ed Bottoms, Robert Peek and Mary Kathryn van Eerden.

Vickie Shufer, Judy Roehling and Lillie Gilbert                    *Photo by Stephanie Herron*

Special thanks to those teachers in Currituck County who assigned history projects to their high school students without whose interviews of community elders, much local knowledge would have been lost. Pilot George Ramsey made it possible to have aerial photographs for this book, providing historical commentary as the various flights were made over these waterways. Thanks to all of the paddlers who accompanied us for one or more river trips: Linda Knowles, Geney Ross, Stephanie Herron, BeeDee McMillan, Margaret McLaughlin, George Ramsey, Bill Spaur, Natalie Ross, Donna and John Gillikin, Jay Wadsworth, Paul Shufer, Joe Gilbert, Barb Francisco, Russ Hawkins, Sandy Baylor, Rhonda Morris, Peggy Fuller, Ginger Sikes, Susie Johnston, Byron Carmean, Jim and Mary Barnes and Judy Roehling, who also acted as note taker when she accompanied us.

The librarians of the Camden/Pasquotank Library, Elizabeth City, North Carolina provided "above-and-beyond" assistance in pulling together history books, maps ands other resources. Pati Terry accompanied me to the library and spent the greater part of a day copying information, scanning maps and photocopying other information. Thanks to our patient husbands, Joe Gilbert and Paul Shufer, for listening to ideas and understanding that a lot of travel was involved in these river trips. Thanks to Paul Shufer for his skilled pre-press expertise and graphics abilities. Proofreaders include W. Michael Lane (Izaak Walton League of America, Suffolk-Nansemond Chapter, VA), Cindy Lane, Randy Jones, Ed Bottoms, Ed Schiller, Joe Gilbert, Patti Gilbert, Doug Gilbert, Deni Norred-Williams, REB Stewart, Bill Petree, Theresa Cherry. Thanks to everyone who encouraged us to complete this book. It means a lot to have your support.

George Ramsey and Lillie Gilbert, preflight                    *Photo by Stephanie Herron*

# Preface

The first time I ever paddled a canoe was into Lake Drummond in the Great Dismal Swamp. The second place I ever paddled a canoe was on Tulls Bay in Currituck County, North Carolina. The waterways in this second book hold a special place in my heart, not only for the nostalgia of my original paddling days, but for the fine friendships that developed from such fabulous recreation. Canoeing was the preferred form of exploring for my paddling buddies and me in the 1970's. My first attempt at kayaking in the late 1970's was with my brand-new Quest kayak on the Lynnhaven River in Virginia Beach near where I live. My kayak arrived before the paddle did so I duct-taped two canoe paddles together and off I went.

Summer weekends were spent in Currituck County. My good friends Ginny and Keith Holsen owned property on Tulls Bay that had been in Ginny's family since the late 1800's. Ginny's two sons, Bobby and Ned Williams were very interested in redoing the old 1930's hunting cabin on the property. The "Shack" as we all lovingly call it, got a new roof, cedar shingles for the sides, new paint in the kitchen and a repaired front porch and screens. All of our friends took turns at various tasks every time we went to the "Shack" for a weekend. Pretty soon it was the favorite place to be for many, many years. It was right on the bay and we swam, paddled, sailed our Hobie Cats, water-skied, fished, flew kites, played volleyball, and cooked some fabulous meals that were eaten on that wonderful old front porch with the incredible view.

By boat, we explored every nearby waterway and got to know the area more by water than by land, much like the early settlers. So, this part of North Carolina feels very much like home and I love the fresh air, the cool mornings, beautiful sunsets, friendly people, blackwater creeks, swamps, rivers and bays, and the colorful history of these waterfront communities.

*Lillie Gilbert*

Dismal Swamp has intrigued me since I first came to Virginia Beach in 1979. My husband Paul and I were eager to explore it. So one Saturday morning, using the "Bicentennial Map of the Great Dismal Swamp" which we had obtained from the U.S. Fish and Wildlife Service, we set out to see what we could find. Aiming for Washington Ditch, which the proposed plans showed to have a visitor center and walking trail, we drove up and down White Marsh Road. That was before signs had been put up and all we could find were dirt roads that led through private farm fields to woods off in the distance. After stopping at a local gas station and asking for directions, we were sent over to "Highway 17" where we were told we could rent a canoe and paddle into the swamp, which we did. We paddled up the Feeder Ditch, crossed the spillway and made it to the lake. Seeing it for the first time, a three thousand acre lake surrounded by forest, was amazing. I wanted to explore more of the swamp and ended up taking a class at Old Dominion University from Dr. Gerald Levy and became an official "swamp rat," as the tour guides were called. This led to doing other programs in the swamp for various groups, including summer camps for teenagers. I got to know the swamp intimately and loved it. In 1998, I presented a paper at the Dismal Swamp Symposium on Ethnobotany.

Exploring the Northwest River and the waterways of northeastern North Carolina has been very much like exploring my backyard due to their proximity. Paddling the waterways has been an extension of land based activities and programs which I have done for a number of years at various locations, including Northwest River Park and Triple R Ranch, both located on the Northwest River. Like trails, each waterway is different and has something unique to offer. It is with pleasure that I've been given the opportunity to work on this Wild River Guide with Lillie and hope it helps others feel and appreciate the beauty of the Dismal Swamp water trails as it has me.

*Vickie Shufer*

# Part One

# Albemarle &

# Chesapeake Canal

*Whereas the opening of a communication of the waters of Elizabeth River with those of North [Landing] River will be of great benefit and advantage ...*
— Hening, Statutes, 11:332-34
from *Juniper Waterway*, 1981

# Albemarle & Chesapeake Canal

The Albemarle and Chesapeake Canal (A&C), like the Dismal Swamp Canal, was an idea conceived by government and completed by private industry. The A&C Canal allows for the connection of the Chesapeake Bay in Virginia to the Albemarle Sound in North Carolina. Connecting waterways include the Elizabeth River, North Landing River, Currituck Bay, and the North Carolina Cut of the Intracoastal Waterway to the North River which empties into Albemarle Sound. This inland passage is a vital north/south link that has allowed the transport of people and products for nearly one hundred and fifty years.

Both the Dismal Swamp Canal and the A&C Canal operate today as alternate routes of the Atlantic Intracoastal Waterway (ICW) and both routes connect the Chesapeake

## Location

Following a west to east direction from Great Bridge in Chesapeake, Virginia, to the North Landing River Drawbridge in Virginia Beach, the Albemarle and Chesapeake Canal, formerly an independent business venture, is now a section of the Intracoastal Waterway from the Southern Branch of the Elizabeth River to the North Landing River.

## Access Point

A.  Route 165/North Landing Road, Virginia Beach, VA

B.  Great Bridge Lock Park, Chesapeake, VA

Pleasure boat on A&C Canal

Bay with the Albemarle Sound. Both canals originate from the waters of the Southern Branch of the Elizabeth River (of which Deep Creek is a tributary) and both have locks to accommodate the water depth differences in the waters at each end. The City of Chesapeake, Virginia is home to more deep-water canals than any city in the United States. Chesapeake's Department of Public Works maintains seventy-seven bridges and overpasses and three drawbridges. The moveable drawbridges operate on a 24-hour basis and open an estimated 23,000 times a year for a wide variety of water vessels (City of Chesapeake, 2001). The A&C Canal's Great Bridge Locks open on the hour, 6 A.M. to 7 P.M. and on demand after 7 P.M. The A&C Canal is maintained and operated by the U.S. Army Corps of Engineers at the Great Bridge Locks and can be reached at (757) 547-2109.

Great Bridge Locks                                                                        lg

In writing about this area in the 1730's, William Byrd II said that south of Norfolk the frontier began (Fischer and Kelly, 2000). By 1878, when Nathaniel Bishop, founder of the American Canoe Association in 1880, made his remarkable canoe trip from Quebec to Florida, he described the area in much the same way. "A few miles [past] Norfolk the cultivation of land ceases, and the canoeist traverses a wilderness" (Bishop, 1878).

Today, much of the land bordering the man-made canal, called the "Virginia Cut," is still undeveloped and tall pines and underbrush mask the quickly spreading city of Chesapeake. The fully dredged length of the A&C

Canal continues into the North Landing River at Virginia Beach, Virginia, crosses the state line at Mile 33.9 into North Carolina and is the route of the Atlantic Intracoastal Waterway. The "North Carolina Cut" begins near Coinjock, North Carolina at Mile 48.3. This man-made canal, more than five miles long, ends at the North River. Following the North River to its juncture with the Albemarle Sound, ICW day marker 173 marks the southern terminus of the A&C Canal. This marker, set on pilings, is the site of a former lighthouse. For more information about the North River, see pages 149-155.

While originally designed for commerce, the Canal today is also used by the many pleasure boaters traveling from north to south in winter and the reverse in spring and summer months. In 2002, along the part of the waterway at Wrightsville Beach (out of the scope of this book, but a part of the Intracoastal Waterway), it was noted that of the nearly 8,000 vessels that required a raising of the drawbridge, only 800 to 1,000 were commercial or government vessels (La Vere, 2003). The remainder were pleasure craft and the boats that did not require any opening of the bridge were the smaller canoes, kayaks, and motorized small boats that were not counted. As in the early days, constant maintenance is required from the silting that builds up. In North Carolina along the entire course of the waterway, $4 to 5 million a year is spent on dredging (La Vere, 2003). Hopefully funds will always be available to this vital link in our country's chain of waterways to keep them free-flowing and deep enough for the varied traffic, whether commercial, military or recreational.

North Carolina Cut

*vs*

# Access Points

## A. Route 165/North Landing Road, Virginia Beach, VA

*Directions*: From the Virginia Beach courthouse, go south on Route 165/North Landing Road, approximately 3¼ miles. Near the drawbridge over the Albemarle & Chesapeake (A&C) Canal, we usually use the boat ramp on the northeast side of the bridge. It is possible to paddle under the drawbridge if desired. There is also a grassy field bordering the upper North Landing River on the west side of North Landing Road. The residents in the last house before the bridge are the owners and will let you park and launch your canoe or kayak for a small fee. To get to the Albemarle and Chesapeake Canal, paddle east under the bridge and around the boat launching area to the North Landing River. Go west, under the drawbridge and you will be on the A&C Canal.

Launch site at North Landing River Drawbridge                                    *vs*

## B. Great Bridge Lock Park, Chesapeake, VA

*Directions*: There is a boat ramp at **Great Bridge Lock Park**, a spacious Chesapeake city park, located on the Intracoastal Waterway, just off Route 168/Battlefield Boulevard. Turn west on Locks Road and drive to the end of the park. Put in at the ramp on the eastern side of the Great Bridge Lock Park.

*Facilities*: **Great Bridge Lock Park**, with 19.7 acres, contains restrooms, a children's playground and picnic tables. A boat ramp with plenty of parking is available for daytime use. Bleachers have been set up for spectators to watch the many working vessels and pleasure craft that utilize the lock.

# Paddling Sections

1. North Landing River Drawbridge to Great Bridge Lock Park

2. Great Bridge Lock Park to Southern Branch of the Elizabeth River

## Section 1. (A) North Landing River Drawbridge to (B) Great Bridge Lock Park – 8½ miles. Chesapeake, VA

This 8½ mile journey along the Albemarle and Chesapeake Canal is interesting because of its history and its glimpse into the plant communities that grow close to the riverbanks. On the east side of the bridge, the North Landing River forms the boundary between Chesapeake and Virginia Beach. West of the bridge, the entire canal is in Chesapeake. To further confuse the vehicle driver, North Landing Road changes names to Mount Pleasant Road on the Chesapeake side, but remains Route 165. See map below. The journey by canoe or kayak from this point south is fully described in our first river book, *Wild River Guide to the North Landing River and Its Tributaries.*

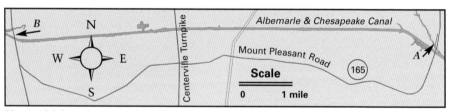

**Map 1:** A&C Canal from North Landing River Drawbridge to Great Bridge Lock Park    © Vickie Shufer

## River Highlights

The "little pines" mentioned by Bishop in 1878 (see page 25) have been logged and replaced with bald cypress and water tupelo trees in the low wet areas. A rookery on the north side has been established by great blue herons and great egrets which can frequently be seen flying overhead. Ospreys build their nests in the tops of old trees and occasionally a bald eagle can be seen resting on the branches.

A power line intersects the canal about 3½ miles west of the drawbridge and is a good spot to get out and stretch your legs. To the north is an old growth forest with bald cypress trees up to twenty-two feet in circumference. Most of this land is owned by The Nature Conservancy. Also, in the mid-1900's, The Virginia Outdoors Foundation (VOF) acquired a donation of a perpetual conservation easement on a tract of private property in this area. Continuing west, you will pass **Camp Baker Boy Scout Camp** on the north side. Less than a mile from the locks is the **Atlantic Yacht Basin.**

# Voyage of the Paper Canoe

In 1874, Nathaniel H. Bishop bought an 18-foot, 300-pound wooden canoe and with an assistant, left Quebec on a historic canoe trip. After 400 miles, in Troy, New York, he dismissed his assistant, purchased a 58-pound solo canoe, and for 2000 more miles paddled the connecting waterways of the East Coast. The lightweight canoe was created from state-of-the-art paper and varnished to make it completely watertight. It was almost completely decked and designed to be either rowed or paddled.

Bishop spent the night of December 4, 1874 at a hotel in Norfolk after storing his canoe at the Old Dominion Steamship Company. He began his trip along the "frontier" the next morning. He describes the river trip in his publication *Voyage of the Paper Canoe*, 1878.

*About noon I arrived at the locks of the Albemarle and Chesapeake Canal. The telegraph operator greeted me with the news that the company's agent in Norfolk had telegraphed to the lock-master to pass the paper canoe through the freedom of the canal – the first honor of the kind that had fallen my lot. The tide rises and falls at the locks in the river about three feet and a half. When I passed through, the difference in the level between the ends of the locks did not reach two feet. The old lock-master urged me to give up my journey at once, as I never could 'get through the Sounds with that little boat.' When I told him that I was on my second thousand miles of canoe navigation since leaving Quebec, he drew a long breath and gave a low groan.*

*When once through the canal-gates, you are in a heavy cypress swamp. The dredgings thrown upon the banks have raised the edge of the swamp to seven feet above the water. Little pines grow along these shores, and among them the small birds, now on their southern migrations, sported and sang. Whenever a steamer or tugboat passed me, it crowded the canoe close to the bank; but these vessels travel along the canal at so slow a rate, that no trouble is experienced by the canoeist from the disturbance caused by their revolving screws. Freedmen, poling flats loaded with shingles or frame stuff, roared out their merry songs as they passed. The canal entered the North Landing River without any lockage; just beyond was North Landing, from which the river takes its name. A store and evidences of a settlement meet the eye at a little distance. The river is torturous, and soon leaves the swamp behind. The pine forest is succeeded by marshes on both sides of the slow-moving current* (Reprinted, Courtesy of Coastal Carolina Press).

## Section 2. (B) Great Bridge Lock Park to Southern Branch of the Elizabeth River – mileage variable. Chesapeake, VA

By paddling northwest from the park, the paddler has several interesting places to explore. About ¼ mile from the boat ramp look for the first small creek to the south and paddle to the end. Even though the Chesapeake Municipal Center looms in the background, there are often many birds to be seen. On our last trip, horses were grazing lazily by the little inlet. The water is quite clear allowing paddlers to see many small fish. A large area of wetlands just west of this site has recently been preserved as part of the compensatory wetland mitigation package for development planned for property north of the river (contact Corps of Engineers for more information).

A southwesterly turn into a large oxbow of the river, less than ½ mile from the boat ramp, leads into Bells Mill Creek. There are wading birds and a fairly healthy looking marsh although there is waterfront industry nearby. There is at least one partially submerged abandoned ship in the oxbow and a lunch spot on the island that was created by the river and oxbow.

Continuing west out of the oxbow, it is preferable to stay near the shoreline, as this is a frequently traveled commercial shipping route. We usually see at least one fisherman so there may be an opportunity to do some casting near some of the small inlets. There are some large homes built on the

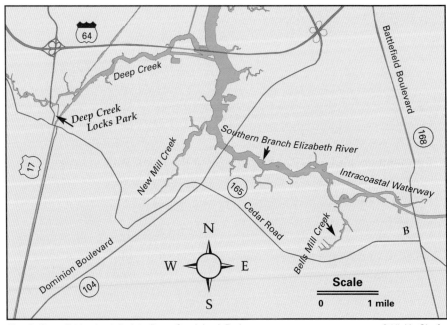

**Map 2:** Great Bridge Lock Park to Deep Creek Lock Park      © Vickie Shufer

north shore and the boat ramps are private. There is no public access so judge the paddling time and plan for a return trip to the park before dark. There are fewer homes on the southern side of the river and much of the scenery still appears natural.

Approximately 4 miles from the boat ramp and ½ mile past the Dominion Boulevard Bridge (formerly Route 104, now U.S. 17) is the entrance to New Mill Creek. Paddle this creek before all of its surrounding land is developed. A little over two miles long, this is the last creek along this side of the Elizabeth River before Deep Creek and its locks that mark the entrance to the Dismal Swamp Canal.

## Saltmarshes

The saltmarshes you see bordering the Elizabeth River and its tributaries experience high and low tides each day. These marshes benefit the ecosystem in many ways. Stands of saltmarsh cordgrass growing along the water's edge act as a buffer by helping to prevent erosion while the spongy, nutrient-rich soil helps to prevent flooding by slowly absorbing and releasing water. As the grasses die and break down they add nutrients to the water. Rails, coots and other marsh birds find shelter and food among the grasses. Fiddler crabs can be seen scurrying around at low tide. When approached they quickly duck into their burrows in the mud. They are preyed upon by various wading birds, including herons and egrets. Periwinkle snails can be spotted on the grasses where they feed on algal growth or on the grasses themselves. They also provide food for a number of birds.

## Waltonian Park – Izaak Walton League Site

The Waltonian Park is a 40+ acre site owned by the Norfolk-Chesapeake Chapter of the Izaak Walton League of America that borders Deep Creek on Shipyard Road in Chesapeake, Virginia. The park provides various services to the community and offers camping, fishing and boating for members and guests. The purpose of the Izaak Walton League is to conserve, maintain, protect and restore the soil, forest, water and other natural resources; educational programs are made available to schools and libraries.

On the site are a number of rare and interesting plants, including galax, mountain laurel, witch-hazel, sweetleaf and highbush blueberry. A mature hardwood forest with oaks and hickories extends beyond the salt marsh that borders Deep Creek.

For more information, call (757) 487-2912.

## Elizabeth River Project

From Great Bridge Lock Park to the Naval Base in Portsmouth, Virginia, the Elizabeth River Project is involved in a major clean-up effort for one of the most polluted rivers in the country. By working with legislators, admirals, heads of businesses and environmental groups, they hope "to restore the Elizabeth River to the highest practical level of environmental quality through government, business and community partnerships" by restoring wetlands and reducing toxins entering into the river. For membership information, call 757-399-7487 (RIVR).

Southern Branch of the Elizabeth River at Bells Mill Creek                    *lg*

# History

The A&C Canal was originally known as the Chesapeake and Albemarle Canal and was actually authorized by Virginia fifteen years before the Dismal Swamp Canal. Work was begun only after a series of delays. During the first delay caused by the Revolutionary War, interestingly enough, the first land battle on Virginia soil took place at Great Bridge. In 1775 British troops, under the direction of Lord Dunmore, were defeated by the colonists and sent back to Norfolk. They remained in Norfolk for only two days and then boarded ships, never to return to Great Bridge. This first victory of the Revolution enabled the Americans to use the waters of the Chesapeake Bay for five years until the British regained a foothold in 1779. It was near this battle site, that in 1859 the single lock of the A&C Canal with reversible gate heads, probably the first of their kind, was built to allow ships to lock up or down depending on the water level. This lock was 220 feet long, 40 feet wide and 8 feet deep. It was the second largest lock chamber in North America and the world's first reversible head lock.

Marshall Parks, Jr. (1820-1900), was president of the Albemarle and Chesapeake Canal Company for nearly thirty years. His father was by 1835 an agent for some of the steamboat lines that utilized the Dismal Swamp Canal. The elder Parks had also been superintendent and chief engineer of the Dismal Swamp Canal Company, so the younger Parks had an early education in maritime activities. He left school at fifteen to help out in his father's milling businesses in South Mills, VA (Brown, 1981). By 1840 when his father died, Parks, Jr. at age twenty, became associated with the construction of steam vessels to be used along the Dismal Swamp Canal. Fully realizing the lengthy traveling time spent by ships on the Dismal Swamp Canal, sometimes as long as twenty days to reach Elizabeth City, Parks understood that the extensive locking system was inordinately slow. In times of drought, the Canal even had to be shut down completely.

Engineering wonder that it was, the Dismal Swamp Canal, with the towing, poling, and pushing methods of transport along the footpath, coupled with waits for the locks, simply took too long for goods to reach markets. Another canal was proposed in 1850 by Parks' ally, Hon. Henry A. Wise, at a meeting in Norfolk to be "at the head of the east fork of the South Branch of the Elizabeth River, a few miles above Great Bridge" extending to the Currituck and Albemarle Sounds in North Carolina

(Brown, 1981). This route had been discussed as early as 1772 when a study was made to determine whether the canal should go through the Elizabeth River's Eastern or Southern Branch.

The beginning of work on the Dismal Swamp Canal (DSC) in 1763, the War of 1812, lack of interest and lack of funds further delayed the building of the A&C. By 1854, numerous congressional acts had been passed enabling construction and in 1855 actual work finally began. A total of $800,000 in stock was officially authorized and Marshall Parks, Jr. began contracting out the mammoth task. While the DSC was dug largely with slave labor, the A&C was dug with nine steam dredges which operated on floating platforms. Seven of the dredges worked in Virginia and two in North Carolina. Said Edmund Ruffin, botanist and writer and sometimes editor of the *Farmer's Register* in Petersburg, in describing the work at North Landing:

> ... *the very low swamp just above the bridge. The earth was barely above the water, and covered with heavy and thick swamp forest growth - and beneath the surface, in the former channel of the river, were buried numerous sound stumps and trunks of cypress trees, which had been covered deeply by the slow accumulation of vegetable soil for ages past. The cutting through and removal of this mass of dead (but sound) wood, embedded in semi-fluid mire, and beneath standing water, could scarcely have been effected at all, except by the wonderful machines in use, which derives aid from the presence of deep water, in which no hand-labor could effect anything* (Ruffin, 1861).

Completed in just four years, the canal created by the steam-driven technology was an engineering marvel.

The opening of the new canal in 1859 gave owners of the DSC serious cause for worry. The A&C was the shorter of the two routes and thus received most of the boat traffic. Although both canals coexisted for fifty-four years, the DSC could not compete when in 1912 the government bought the A&C and removed the tolls. As bankruptcy loomed for the DSC, the government bought its second canal in the area in 1929. Today, the U.S. Army Corps of Engineers operates both canals toll-free.

---

*The Atlantic seaboard's Albemarle and Chesapeake Canal, connecting the sound and bay for which it is jointly named, is one of the nation's most beautiful as well as most useful artificial waterways.*

– Alexander Crosby Brown, 1981

# Part Two

# Dismal Swamp Canal

*I have long been satisfied of the practicability of opening communication between the waters which empty into Albemarle sound thro' Drummond's Pond and the Waters of Elizabeth or Nansemond Rivers.*

– George Washington, March 31, 1784
from *The Dismal Swamp Canal*
by Alexander Crosby Brown, 1971

# Dismal Swamp Canal

While paddling the entire length of today's twenty-two mile canal may be a formidable task, it is possible to break the trip into many interesting parts. Because of its uniqueness and historical significance, we truly believe the Dismal Swamp Canal (DSC), or part of it, should be included on every paddler's life list.

## Access Points

### (A) Deep Creek Lock Park, Chesapeake, VA

There is no designated canoe or kayak launch site, but a paddler's informal access would be the low bank on the shoreline at the gravel parking lot. Look along the water's edge and find an appropriate spot near the entrance of the park/parking area. The paddler is now in that portion of the Intracoastal Waterway known as the Dismal Swamp Canal.

*Directions:* The **Deep Creek Lock Park** is located at 300 Luray Street, just north of the intersection of U.S. 17/George Washington Highway and Route 165/Cedar Road in Chesapeake, Virginia.

**Location**

The Dismal Swamp Canal begins in the Deep Creek section of Chesapeake, Virginia and connects the waters of Hampton Roads, the Elizabeth River and the southern Chesapeake Bay with the waters of North Carolina's Joyce Creek, the Pasquotank River and the Albemarle Sound to the south.

**Access Points**

A. Deep Creek Lock Park, VA

B. Great Dismal Swamp Boat Ramp, VA

C. Dismal Swamp Canal Visitor Information Center, NC

D. SR 1211/ Joy's Creek Road

E. SR 1211/ Bingham Road

**Note:** To meet the safety needs of 21st Century traffic, Virginia is currently re-routing and upgrading U.S. 17 along a new alignment, located approximately ½ mile to the east of the existing road. Originally, plans were to expand the existing 2-lane road to a 4-lane divided highway along the canal bank. However, local citizens, conservation, historical preservation and outdoor recreation groups (Izaak Walton League, Sierra Club, Great Dismal Swamp Coalition, Virginia Canals and Navigation Society, Tidewater

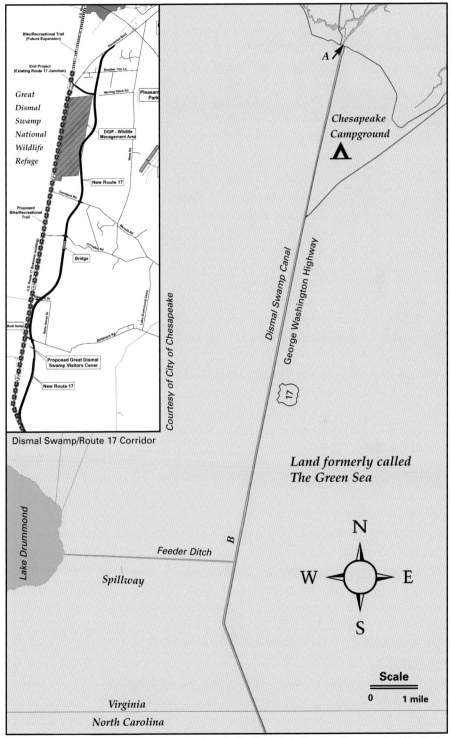

**Map 3:** Dismal Swamp Canal from Deep Creek to the Virginia/North Carolina line     © Vickie Shufer

Bicycle Asociation) became alarmed at the prospect of the potential environmental and aesthetic impacts, as well as the potential to degrade the cultural and historical resources associated with the DSC. At their urging, and through federal environmental regulatory agencies, the location was shifted to the new route now under construction.

Subsequently, the Virginia Department of Game and Inland Fisheries acquired a 750+ acre wooded area between the existing and the new road alignment, south of Dominion Boulevard, now Route 17, and north of Cornland Road, for use as a wildlife management area. Also, the city of Chesapeake is exploring ways of converting the present 2-lane road to a multi-use scenic and recreational trail. These actions will preserve and significantly enhance the scenic and recreational attributes of the DSC. All references in this guide to U.S. 17 in Virginia along DSC refer to the 20th century location of the road.

*Facilities:* **Deep Creek Lock Park**, maintained by the City of Chesapeake Parks and Recreation, is open from sunrise to sunset. It is named for the U.S. Army Corps of Engineers' lock that was designated a National Historic Engineering Landmark in 1987 by the American Society of Civil Engineers. The lock separates the salty water of Deep Creek from the fresh water of the Dismal Swamp Canal. The lock opens four times a day: 8:30 A.M., 11:00 A.M., 1:30 P.M. and 3:30 P.M. Amenities at the park include playground equipment, picnic tables, portable toilet, drinking water and parking for at least 45 cars. This wooded park has walking trails in the woods, a pedestrian bridge and elevated walkways in the marsh and tidal inlet.

*Camping:* On U.S. 17, two miles south of the Deep Creek drawbridge is the **Chesapeake Campground** at 693 South George Washington Highway, Chesapeake, Virginia 23323. This privately-owned 100-acre farm and campground is open year-round and has many amenities including canoe rentals. There is a small clearing adjacent to the canal which can be used as an access point for paddlers. Do ask for permission. Across the highway is the country store run by the campground. This makes a comfortable stop for refreshments. For complete details, call (757) 485-0149.

## (B) Great Dismal Swamp Boat Ramp, Chesapeake, VA

*Directions:* From I-64 take Route 104/Dominion Boulevard west to U.S. 17 /George Washington Highway and go south approximately 14 miles. The boat ramp is on the west side of U.S. 17 near the intersection of West Ballahack Road in Chesapeake, Virginia. This is a paved ramp with plenty of parking. The no-fee public launch site contains no restroom facilities.

## Safety Tip

The Intracoastal Waterway is the route of the motor yacht delivery crews who may not be watching for kayaks or canoes at the edges of the waterway. Bill Spaur, who is a frequent paddler on the DSC, likes to "row just outside the navigation aids on my correct side of the channel. I may move a little into the channel if wake-making motor boats are approaching. I do not do this with tugs pushing barges. I pull for shallow water where they cannot get me. Barges cannot be stopped nor maneuvered. They will have to run over you if you are in the channel." Items of importance to have on board include a horn, marine VHF radio, and GPS.

# (C) Visitor Information Center, Dismal Swamp Canal

*Directions:* Continue south on U.S. 17 from Chesapeake, Virginia. On the drive to the Visitor Center in North Carolina, the traveler crosses the DSC on U.S. 17 via the towering William Ira Halstead Bridge, constructed in 1982. This bridge is 2,132 feet long with a vertical clearance of 65 feet, offering a superb panoramic view of the countryside and the historic canal.

Paddlers looking for the put-in need only to venture to the south end of the parking lot near the canal. Look for the sign, "Canoe Access," offload canoe or kayak, and park in the large parking area nearby. There is a gravel path that leads to the access site at a low spot between the high spoil banks. Sandy soil at the water's edge and a break in the old bulkhead allows for extremely easy access.

Visitor Information Center, Dismal Swamp Canal                                     *lg*

*Facilities:* The DSC Visitor Information Center has a gift shop that is open 9-5:00 P.M. seven days a week from Memorial Day through October 31, and Tuesday though Saturday from November 1st to Memorial Day weekend. A dock for motorized craft is very near the Visitor Center and north of the canoe/kayak access site. This 150-foot shoreline dock is available for sailboats and motor yachts to use as an overnight stop. No fishing or swimming is allowed from the dock.

Other amenities are large parking areas, restrooms, drinking water, vending machines for drinks and snacks, picnic tables, a public telephone, pet exercise area and the launch site for non-motorized craft. Charcoal grills and picnic areas are available for all guests. The staff of the center is very friendly, knowledgeable and helpful. They have given rides into nearby areas for boaters seeking groceries or medical assistance and have an Internet port to be used with toll-free telephone numbers. Home-schooled children traveling with their parents by boat have even used their Internet service. A paperback book exchange is provided for visitors who need a change of reading material.

## *President Andrew Jackson on the DSC*

Following a celebrated visit to Norfolk on July 9, 1829, President Andrew Jackson paid a visit to the Dismal Swamp Canal. A reporter for a New York newspaper was quoted in the *American Beacon* July 29, 1829:

*"... (I) saw the President enter the Canal in a barge sent thither by the Navy Yard at Gosport. He descended into the locks, and then was brought up to the level and conveyed by means of a rope attached to one of the carriages, six miles, which afforded at that point, a full view of the Canal, as far as the eye could reach. The party debarked, and a collation was immediately spread on the table, made of cypress shingles ... The President of the United States and the other gentlemen were each provided with a clean shingle which answered for a plate. The servants handed around slices of Virginia ham, smoked beef and tongues, and every one immediately set to work to demolish a good portion of the things which had been so kindly provided. General Jackson said it put him in mind of old times; that he had often taken his meals on a log in the woods, and always with a good appetite. The fresh air and exercise, he observed, were the best sauces; everything was truly excellent; all seemed ready for the repast ..."* (Emmerson, 1949).

Aerial view of South Mills Locks and Joyce Creek in upper right                    lg

# (D) SR 1211/Joy's Creek Road

*Directions:* In South Mills, NC, at the east side of the U.S. 17 bridge over the Dismal Swamp Canal, turn south on SR 1211/Joy's Creek Road. Drive past the locks until an easy spot to launch can be located. There are many mowed places right next to the canal that are easily accessible. Please do not park on private property.

A good spot to refuel one's vehicle or one's self is the convenience store and snack bar at the Exxon Station on U.S. Business 17 on the northwest side of the bridge in South Mills. This is the site of the former inn, Bullock's Tavern.

# (E) SR 1211/Bingham Road

*Directions:* Bingham Road is a southerly continuation of SR 1211 and the name changes from Joy's Creek Road to Bingham shortly after the Joyce Creek Bridge. It is interesting to note that the names of the creek and the road have different spellings. Information on Joyce Creek is on page 175.

# The Canal's Early Beginnings

The Dismal Swamp Canal (DSC) was originally dug by hand with construction starting from both ends, Virginia and North Carolina. While the canal would become a major artery of transportation of various goods, the first intent was to allow the removal of timber from the Dismal Swamp. Of the valuable commodities made from cypress and cedar, shingles were to be the big moneymaker, feeding the building boom of a fast growing nation. Shingles and other timber resources were removed from the Dismal Swamp and transported by water, as roads in the area were few and unsatisfactory for the heavy loads. Canal work was begun in 1793 and continued until 1805 when the Dismal Swamp Canal was opened for the limited transport of flat-bottom boats and log rafts. To recover the costs of construction and to repay the various stockholders, the canal company charged tolls.

The first hostelry was established in 1802 along the canal. The owner, William Farange, located his establishment about 2 ½ miles south of the VA/NC border on part of the 50 acres he had purchased in Camden County (Brown, 1970).

A towpath for two-legged or four-legged haulers to pull the flat bottom lighters that would carry timber products and other commodities was constructed on the high ground next to the canal. Later this towpath would be enlarged to become a stage coach route.

In the 1820's the Dismal Swamp Canal was enlarged to allow shoal-draft boats. The connection between the Chesapeake Bay via the Elizabeth River and the Albemarle Sound via its northern river tributary, the Pasquotank, was a reality. The canal was maintained by a series of locks fed by the Feeder Ditch.

In May of 1826 the governor of Virginia, John Tyler, along with two distinguished members of the state government, Colonel Pendleton, of the Executive Council, and Colonel Crozet, Engineer of the Board of Public Works, arrived in Norfolk by steamer from Richmond. They were anxious to see the Dismal Swamp Canal and visited it on May 16, 1826, accompanied by Directors of the Canal Company and several Norfolkians. As reported in the *Norfolk and Portsmouth Herald*, the future President "expressed great pleasure and admiration at the magnitude and importance of the Canal, which far exceeded his expectations" (Emmerson, 1949). Apparently the canal did not meet all expectations as another canal was planned to extend from "Lynnhaven Creek into the head of Currituck Sound, down the sound" with several other canals to be built to connect rivers and eventually have its terminus at Charleston, South Carolina (Emmerson, 1949).

These plans were submitted in February of 1828 by Chancellor Livingston, Mr. Robert Fulton (civil engineer and inventor of the steamboat) and Mr. Bowden, but the project never materialized. The plan was to dig a canal four miles across Princess Anne County to the proposed canal at the headwaters of the Eastern Branch of the Elizabeth River in Kempsville (Brown, 1981). Imagine what the Lynnhaven and Kempsville areas in present-day Virginia Beach would be like if this project had been completed. It was not until the 1940's that the Lynnhaven was connected to the North Carolina waters by way of the dredging and channeling of West Neck Creek to connect the North Landing River with London Bridge Creek, part of the Eastern Branch of the Lynnhaven River.

## *Age of Steam*

By the late 1820's the age of steam had arrived in the Dismal Swamp Canal, when widening and deepening of the canal and its working lock systems allowed deeper draft and larger boats to travel safely along an inside passage instead of the ships traveling dangerously along the Atlantic coastline. The risks were great as the steamers bringing goods to and from the southern states were sometimes caught off guard with storms and shoals. The "Graveyard of the Atlantic" claimed many souls, ships and valuable cargo. This wonderful canal would then save lives, time and money.

The first steam-propelled vessel traveled the Canal in 1829. A newspaper article from the *Norfolk and Portsmouth Herald* dated January 16 of that year gives credit to the *Elizabeth City Star* for reporting the arrival via the Dismal Swamp Canal of, "a steam boat built of sheet iron, 16 feet wide and 50 feet long, intended to run between Newbern and Beaufort, through the Clubfoot and Harlow Creek canal" (Emmerson, 1949). This steamer had a draft of 2.5 feet. This first steamer was probably the *Cordorus*, a ship that was noted by the *American Beacon* in the shipping news of January 1, 1829 as "at anchor in the mouth of Mill Creek [near the Deep Creek Lock]...bound to Newbern" (Emmerson, 1949). The historic passage marks the start of the many steamboats to ply the Canal's water.

An earlier article (January 2, 1829) printed by the *Norfolk and Portsmouth Herald* tells of the locks allowing enough water into the canal to float the larger draft boats. "We have the pleasure to announce that the water was let into the Canal of Wednesday morning last, to a depth of three and a half, and that for boats of that draught, the navigation is now open. The portion of the embankment which remains to be finished will probably occupy three weeks, when the Canal will be filled. A boat laden with staves, belonging to Mr. Matthew Cluff, of Elizabeth City, has already passed through the Canal, being the first. A number of others, we learn, are on their way through it" (Emmerson, 1949). Mr. Cluff's boat was probably a flat-bottomed boat, easily used for carrying the heavy wooden cargo, not a steamer. Nevertheless, it must have been quite an occasion in January of 1829 to stand on the banks of the canal to see the various craft, including the new steamboats.

## Economic Boon

From 1829 to 1860 the canal and the nearby towns saw the most prosperity. Entrepreneurs in Elizabeth City were aware of the potential of the traffic afforded their city by the Canal. Perfectly situated at the terminus of the Canal's path on the Pasquotank River and on the stage route from Norfolk and Princess Anne County, Elizabeth City was positioned for growth and commerce. The steamers with a shallow draft could travel to the many river and inland bay ports of northeastern North Carolina. One Carolina resident remarked in a letter to the editor of a Norfolk newspaper, "The employment of these boats in our waters presents a new era in the Commerce of the Albemarle. The Agriculturists are looking with intense interest to the success of the [Virginia and North Carolina] Transportation Company" (Emmerson, 1949). The editors of the paper in May of 1829 discussed the desired progress related to the expanding cargo runs from the Roanoke River to the market at Elizabeth City and beyond. "Large streams that have rolled for ages in silence and obscurity to the ocean, shall yet hear the din of commerce – become subservient to industry - and boast delightful villas, gilded spires, and fields loaded with the fruits of cultivation" (Emmerson, 1949).

## Lady of the Lake

A new type of steamer was put into operation in the summer of 1830. Launched from Portsmouth, Virginia at the builder's shipyard, the *Lady of the Lake* was to take her place in history as being the first boat on the Canal "to be propelled by paddles in the stern." This new design was intended to allow the boat to pass through the Canal "without injury to the banks." She was 65 feet long on deck and was built as a tow and passage boat. In July, 1830 the president and three directors of the Dismal Swamp Canal Company, along with Lt. Talcott of the Engineer Corps and newspaper reporters rode on the *Lady of the Lake* all the way to the Pasquotank River. "The result of the experiment entirely satisfied the Directors, that a steam boat, on the plan of the *Lady of the Lake* is less liable to injure the banks by the agitation of the water which her paddles produced, than a vessel propelled by sails, moving with the same velocity; and not more than an ordinary tow boat" (Emmerson, 1949).

Problems arose when the *Lady of the Lake* and other boats would arrive at a North Carolina port and farmers or sellers would not have delivered produce. The low water of summer and shoals of the Albemarle Sound and its rivers often stopped boats of commerce from getting their products to market. The system must have worked itself out as steamers continued arriving in Elizabeth City and the commerce from as far away as Weldon on the Roanoke River eventually made it to the market in Norfolk via the Dismal Swamp Canal. In the March 4, 1831 *Herald*, it states, "We were yesterday gratified with the sight of the steamboat *Lady of the Lake*, crossing our harbor from the canal, with the schnrs. *Imogene* and *Carolina Augusta* in tow. The *Lady of the Lake* took three vessels up through the canal to Weldon, just a fortnight ago, both were laden with merchandise, which were loaded at different places on the Roanoke. At Weldon they took 500 bales of cotton, which they have returned to Norfolk after an absence of only 14 days. The company who are the proprietors of this concern … have in contemplation, as we learn, to build a suitable steamboat to run between Elizabeth City and Weldon, and to reserve the *Lady of the Lake* for a tow boat, to ply between Norfolk and Elizabeth City, through the canal. They will thus be enabled to deliver two boats laden with produce from the Roanoke at Norfolk, at least once a week" (Emmerson, 1949).

In April of 1831, the Virginia and North Carolina Transportation Company and the Lady of the Lake Company decided to form "a union of the two lines." The Committee of Directors decided to utilize three boats in the steam ship operation. As reported by the *Beacon*, the "*Lady of the Lake* will be employed exclusively in towing between Norfolk and Elizabeth City; the *Petersburg* between Elizabeth City and Plymouth, and the *North Carolina* between Plymouth and Weldon. The arrival of the boats at each end may, by this arrangement be calculated to a day" (Emerson, 1949).

On the 26th of November, 1831, the *North Carolina* burned, leaving only two boats to supply the successful freight avenues. The optimism of the canal builders and the owners of the steamboats sadly dwindled as did the water conditions of the 1830s. With traffic from horse drawn boats, poled boats, sailboats, and the steamers, the canal suffered from a variety of problems, including erosion of the canal banks. The *Lady of the Lake* was put up for auction on August 10, 1833. The steamboat *Petersburg* was sold for use on the Roanoke River exclusively.

Meanwhile on the canal and from Portsmouth, pleasure boaters were enjoying trips to look at the locks at Deep Creek and to get a glimpse of the canal from the banks. Other steamers and sail boats as well as flat bottom boats still provided a way to get shingles and produce to market to feed a growing nation. Soon the rumble of railroads would threaten the lifelines of commerce that the canals had become.

## The Dismal Swamp Canal's Role in Wartime

During the Civil War, the canal provided a strategic advantage for the army that controlled it. During the 1862 Union blockade of the Carolina coast, the canal was a supply route and an escape route for Confederate troops heading to Virginia. It is said that the route along the Dismal Swamp Canal and some of the drainage ditches interior to the swamp were also escape routes for those escaping the bonds of slavery, making this part of the Underground Railroad. During the Battle of South Mills, the Union's intent to damage the canal and make it part of the Union's holdings was thwarted. The Union did not want any of the supposed Confederate ironclads to make way down the Dismal Swamp Canal to the waters of the Albemarle Sound. It was thought that this was the route they were to use in order to get much-needed supplies to Confederate troops. Other wartime activities caused severe damage to the DSC. The Canal Company managed to hang on to the canal until 1878 when it was sold. In 1892 the Lake Drummond Canal and Water Company took over the canal and began the rehabilitation project.

## Decline of an Era

Between 1896 and 1899 the original stone locks were replaced by locks of steel, wood and cement. All of the intermediate locks were removed so that there were just two locks: Deep Creek, Virginia and South Mills, North Carolina. During this three year "Great Improvement," the width of the Canal was doubled, the towpath was done away with, the Canal was dug to a six foot controlling depth, and the water level was changed at the Feeder Ditch dam. It is suspected that during this time, the original stone mileage markers were moved (Ramsey, 2001).

Despite all of this expensive work, the undoing of the Dismal Swamp Canal occurred shortly after the turn of the twentieth century. By 1912 the U.S. Army Corps of Engineers had bought the Albemarle and Chesapeake Canal and by 1913 removed its tolls. This had a devastating effect on the amount of boat traffic on the Dismal Swamp Canal, as money collected from its tolls was required in order to maintain it. After this time, since it was not used as much, the Dismal Swamp Canal fell into disrepair.

In 1929 the United States bought the Dismal Swamp Canal. The U.S. Army Corps of Engineers took charge of the canal and rebuilt the locks with new ones of concrete and steel. In 1935 a new dam and spillway replaced the lock at Lake Drummond (Brown, 1970). As the canal changed over time to meet its floating demands, the towpath, which first paralleled the Dismal Swamp Canal was destroyed by widening of the canal. The high ground adjacent to the east side of the canal became a stagecoach road before it grew into the current form as the original roadway of U.S. 17. The Dismal Swamp Canal is recognized as a National Civil Engineering Landmark as well as a National Historic Landmark (*North Carolina Atlas and Gazetteer*, 1993).

*The regular "swamper," however, is often a boatman as well as axe man, and the canal is seldom without the sight of a heavy-laden lighter, long and narrow, propelled by its two "trackers" (from the low Dutch "treck"), pushing against long poles fastened, as seen in the sketch, at the bow and stern* (Harpers Weekly, June 14, 1873).

# The Underground Railroad and the Great Dismal Swamp

In this place of many secrets, one of the more interesting is the collection of tales about the "maroon colonies" set up deep in the confines of the Great Dismal Swamp. Although no written records exist to document the numbers of individuals who sought refuge here, historians now believe the communities of escaped slaves were among the largest in the United States (U.S. Fish and Wildlife Service, 2004). If there were ever a place to harbor run-aways, the dense vegetation as well as the inhospitable reputation of the Dismal Swamp would provide the perfect cover. William Byrd reported in 1728, "Some of the neighbors have lost themselves here for some days, but never had the courage or curiosity to advance very far." As early as 1784, swamps were known as a refuge for slaves. John Ferdinand Smyth in *A Tour of the United States* reports, "Run-away slaves have resided in these places for twelve, twenty, or thirty years and upwards, subsisting themselves in the swamps upon corn, hogs, and fowls, that they raised on the spots not perpetually under water, nor subject to be flooded..."

Whether the maroons were a real or perceived threat to locals, a legislative act by the North Carolina State Assembly in 1847 entitled "Act to provide for the apprehension of runaway slaves in the Great Dismal Swamp and for other purposes" was passed. The Civil War brought the African Brigade, as they were known, to Norfolk and Portsmouth under the command of General E. A. Wild. Because both cities were active ports, it is believed that many slaves could have been helped out of the area by sympathetic or opportunistic sea captains. In 1863 Wild was directed to recruit as many former slaves as possible in the area. After the war, historians believed that any non-recruited maroons or "outlyers" had left the swamp.

On February 13, 2004, the Great Dismal Swamp National Wildlife Refuge was officially named as the first refuge to be listed by the National Park Service to the "Underground Railroad Network to Freedom Program." The Dismal Swamp Canal, the Dismal Swamp Canal Visitor Information Center and the Dismal Swamp State Park are also recognized as sites receiving the "National Underground Railroad Network to Freedom Designation."

## Paddling Sections

1. **Deep Creek Lock Park to Great Dismal Swamp Boat Ramp - 10¼ miles**
2. **Great Dismal Swamp Boat Ramp to Dismal Swamp Canal Visitor Center - 7 miles**
3. **Dismal Swamp Canal Visitor Center to SR 1211/ Joy's Creek Road - ⁹⁄₁₀ mile**

## Section 1. (A) Deep Creek Lock Park to (B) Great Dismal Swamp Boat Ramp - 10¼ miles, one way. Chesapeake, VA

Deep Creek is said to have gotten its name from a mishap of one of our country's founding fathers. Local tradition has it that George Washington, while surveying along the creek (or by some accounts while horseback riding along the creek), fell into the water. As he emerged he remarked, "That's a deep creek!" Mr. Washington was a tall man of 6' 2½" so the creek must have made an impression. The name apparently stuck as the creek and community surrounding it still use that name.

Today it is possible to paddle a little over a mile to the west from Deep Creek Lock Park into the area between Old Mill Road and Gallberry Road. If one were to paddle northeast from the park into the larger portion of Deep Creek as it enters the Southern Branch of the Elizabeth River, one would agree that here the water is quite deep.

To paddle south from the lock area puts the boater on the Dismal Swamp Canal. The paddler will first pass under the Deep Creek Bridge, built in 1934. This two lane single bascule span bridge opens on demand, in conjunction with the lock openings, and like the lock, is operated by the U.S. Army Corps of Engineers. After this point the next bridge is the aforementioned William Ira Halstead bridge, 14 miles to the south, in North Carolina.

The Dismal Swamp Canal is a straight line from Deep Creek Lock Park to the Great Dismal Swamp Boat Ramp. The boat ramp is on the east side of the canal. Look for the bulkheaded area and turn into the cut for the ramp.

vs

# The Lock "Chessie" Monster

A recent visitor to the area is a large manatee whom lock attendants at Great Bridge say waits patiently for the locks to fill and then continues on its journey. Nicknamed "Chessie," the manatee drew the attention of one of the authors several years ago when Chessie appeared for the first time. In the summer of 1994, when requested by the Virginia Marine Science Museum to go and look by canoe for the warm water mammal, the author more than willingly complied. We were asked to go to Deep Creek. No manatee was seen, but a wonderful paddling day on the backwaters of Deep Creek was appreciated.

On August 30, 2001, a manatee returned and was this time seen by quite a few people, most notably lock attendants Joel Scussel and Rob Poyner who called Susan Barco, a marine mammal scientist associated with the Virginia Marine Science Museum's stranding Team. (We are proud to report that one of the authors taught Susan when she was in the 6th grade in the Virginia Beach City Public School's Gifted Program. The class was Marine Ecology.) Photographed while in the lock, Chessie was quiet and seemingly undisturbed. By studying the markings and scars it was determined that this was the same Chessie that appeared in 1994, and again in 1995, that time outfitted with a radio locator collar. Chessie had been tracked in the 1995 season as traveling as far north as Rhode Island and then returned to Florida, his place of birth. This West Indian manatee had swum more than 3,000 miles!

On July 17, 1997, Chessie's satellite transmitter was found at Beaufort, South Carolina and the world waited. After a five-year hiatus, Chessie returned to Virginia. We wish Chessie a long life. Please visit the "Chessie Watch Page" on the internet at www.sirenian.org/chessie.html to see pictures of Chessie, our gentleman of the locks; hardly a sea monster at all.

"Chessie"                                                      *Photo courtesy of USGS*

## A Date with Lord Chesterfield

"There is plenty of room for you on the boat," is the message I received from George Ramsey. "And bring a friend, if you like." The boat he was referring to is a wooden shallow draft vessel built just like the 18th century batteaux that ferried commercial cargo on the James River in Virginia. The Virginia Canals and Navigations Society and four of its members had brought the 45-foot replica by trailer to the DSC from Richmond. Similar boats plied the Dismal Swamp Canal carrying human and commercial cargo with the last boat ending the journey in 1899. I had a date with history.

We were to meet at the Deep Creek locks for the opening at 8:30 A.M. and head down the DSC to a rendezvous with Lake Drummond. I asked Vickie if she would like to join me and she jumped at the chance. Realizing that we could not make the starting time, we planned to meet the boat and its period-costumed pilots at about 9:30 A.M. along the Canal at the Chesapeake Campground's launch area. We launched our Kevlar canoe and approached the ancient–looking vessel as the crew slowed the boat to meet us. Seeing the boat for the first time was like suddenly going back in time.

To finally climb aboard, hold the 20-foot pole and propel the craft with human strength was something that propelled us to a different millennium. It was so much more than the Huck Finn experience I thought it would be. "This is our fire box where we do our cooking. These hogsheads are where the cargo is stored," I was told. When I inquired about the economics of such a slow method of transport, I was told that as much as five tons of cargo could be carried on such a vessel. The trip which could take up to three days from Norfolk to Elizabeth City would have taken many more days if attempted overland even if there had been a cargo carrier capable of the weight. It was a dizzying feeling to be immersed in another century's technology and way of life. The *Lord Chesterfield* was a time capsule that transported us not only to a different time, but to a greater appreciation of the river men who earned their living by poling these cumbersome craft along this historic waterway.

*Lillie's Journal Notes, September 28, 2001*

**For more information:** *Virginia Canals and Navigations Society*, 6826 Rosemont Drive, McLean, VA 22101.

## The Mystery of the Stone Markers

vs

It only seems fitting in this unusual place that yet another mystery has presented itself. George Ramsey, Bill Spaur and fellow archaeological sleuths of the **Virginia Canals and Navigations Society** are determined to discover and reset all of the original stone mile markers that were placed along the east side of the DSC. Some of the stones were found in the water and some on land. The stones are large, chiseled, granite monoliths, 76 to 80 inches in length with a width or depth of 10 to 14 inches, numbered in a beautiful style. Estimated weight of each is 1,000 pounds and a total of 11½ have been located so far. All of these found have been placed in their approximate locations along the canal bank. How these stones were transported and how originally erected is unknown. The mile numbers do not correspond to the actual canal miles but are close. While no written record of the stone markers has been found, it is probable that they were erected prior to 1841. No one knows who set them in place or when.

It is interesting to note that the stone markers begin mile zero at the Deep Creek Locks. Today's Army Corps' mile markers for the Intracoastal Waterway begin at Hospital Point on the Elizabeth River between Portsmouth and Norfolk. Not to be confusing, but the marine marker for Mile Zero off Hospital Point in Portsmouth is a red lighted buoy, "36." Today's Deep Creek Lock Army Corps' Mile Marker is number 11 (actually 10.6 statute miles to be exact). So, if using the stone markers as a guide down the Dismal Swamp Canal, the boater needs to add 11 and the 19th century markers will have caught up with the 21st century's reckoning (Ramsey, 2000). Do watch for these mysterious stone markers while boating on the Dismal Swamp Canal.

NW ∨ 15
**DISMAL SWAMP CANAL**

This canal, which connects Chesapeake Bay and Albemarle Sound, was chartered by Virginia in 1787 and North Carolina in 1790. It opened to traffic in 1805 and is now part of the Intracoastal Waterway. The area was visited by William Byrd II in 1728 when he surveyed the boundary between Virginia and North Carolina. In 1763, George Washington explored the area and organized the Dismal Swamp Land Company to drain it for farmland. The Great Dismal Swamp is now a National Wildlife Refuge.

DEPARTMENT OF HISTORIC RESOURCES, 1991

lg

# Historic Sites on or near the Dismal Swamp Canal

The **Wallace House** was known as Mrs. Wallace's Tea Room in the 1930's. This is the last standing structure of the Dismal Swamp Canal Company. The superintendent lived here at the junction of the Northwest River Canal and the Dismal Swamp Canal so he could collect

lg

tolls on both canals. He kept a traffic book to record all of the goods and types of boats that used the canals. The old frame house is closed to the public. Local members of the Virginia Canals and Navigations Society who have a five-year renewable contract with the US Army Corps of Engineers maintain the grounds. The house was built in the early 1800's and, according to the family's oral tradition, the house was moved here from Deep Creek. Just how is unknown (Ramsey, 2001).

The **Lake Drummond Hotel** was opened in January 1830 on the east side of the canal by Isaiah Rogerson. It was advertised first in Norfolk, Virginia as "large and commodious, being 128 feet long and having eight separate chambers, with fireplaces." Its colorful history developed because it was built on the banks of the Dismal Swamp Canal, half in North Carolina and half in Virginia and it became known as the "Halfway House." While it may have been originally designed as a sportsman's lodge, the establishment became known as "a marrying place" for Virginia couples looking for more lenient laws as well as a "house of entertainment" and a dueling spot. North Carolina law-breakers seeking refuge in Virginia had a place to stay as did their counterparts from Virginia who only had to step into the part of the hotel located in North Carolina to avoid capture.

A gentleman on holiday from Scotland in the 1800s wrote, "It was on a cold morning of February that we entered the crazy machine which performs the duty of a 'stage' between Norfolk, Virginia and Elizabeth City, North Carolina … The canal and tall cypress flanked our right, and wild waste-looking corn-fields or tangled bushes our left…It was almost a relief to step into the miserable dining-room of the Halfway House, even though our appetite was too fastidious to be tempted by the bacon and hominy prepared for the travellers" (Simpson, 1990). The hotel passed through several owners and is last mentioned in print in 1850. No trace of the building exists today.

Beechwood House                                                                  lg

**Beechwood**, the William Charles Stewart 1800's plantation home, is located on Belle Haven Street in Chesapeake and is currently uninhabited. William's father-in-law, Henry Garrett, was for many years superintendent of the Dismal Swamp Canal. His son, Robert Edward Bruce Stewart, was born July 20, 1863 and is prominently mentioned in the diary of neighbor, Elizabeth Wallace. The once stately home of the Stewarts now has large pieces of equipment stored in the yard. It is hoped that one day this majestic home will be restored.

**Beechwood** is located within walking distance of the site of the Wallace home, **Glencoe**. An excellent description of the houses of the two friendly families and a day-by-day glimpse into life of these prominent families is the *Glencoe Diary*, the war-time journal of Elizabeth Curtis Wallace, published by the Norfolk County Historical Society of Chesapeake, Virginia and edited by Eleanor P. and Charles B. Cross, Jr. Mrs. Wallace's diary covers events from April, 1863 to December 31, 1864. Mrs. Wallace, then Elizabeth Curtis of Deep Creek, married George Thomas Wallace in 1835. The Wallaces were close friends as well as neighbors of the Stewarts. Their large home, **Glencoe**, used by generations, burned in November of 1979. **Wallaceton** is still listed on some maps and a direct descendant of this family lives in the building on U.S. 17 that served originally as an early post office. This house is across the street from the Northwest Canal. The previously mentioned Superintendent's House (page 50), the last standing structure of the Dismal Swamp Canal Company, is nearby.

The area is extremely rich in history and to read a diary from the Civil War era sheds light on what the local families had to endure, as demonstrated by the following excerpt:

> *Monday, Oct.12, 1863. The Yankees are around us in full force tonight. While we were quietly eating our supper Sam came in and said a man wished to see Mr. Wallace. Mr. W. left the table and a Yankee officer met him at the door and said the Col. Wished to camp here for the night. In a few minutes the premises were surrounded and now half an hour later these heartless invaders are demolishing the fences, destroying the fodder …Camp fires made with our [fence] rails and other timber are burning all around and a guard is walking around the house. I am yet thankful that the same Lord is over us that has provided for and kept us thus far. Tuesday, Oct.13, 1863. Mr. Wallace thinks the soldiers damaged him about 100 dols. They all left at daybreak.*

Three entries are especially interesting in light of the Battle of South Mills which took place nearby a year earlier on April 19, 1862 when Union troops were trying to capture the Dismal Swamp Canal. The local families not bearing arms had been ordered to leave but many were unable or unwilling to leave their homes. The war was literally at their doorsteps.

> *Thursday, April 16, 1863. Fair and mild morning but some rain in the evening. The firing of cannon has continued all day. At twelve o clock today four yankee soldiers came up from Deep Creek and burned the bridge over the N.W. Canal at its junction with the D.S. Canal. Mrs Boush had just crossed over it to go to J. Garretts. In the evening Mrs. Orr and Mrs. Holt asked for accommodations for the night. They reported that Gates County is full of Confederates. A report also came in that orders had been issued to the women and children and all persons not under arms to leave Norfolk & Portsmouth; also that the Confederates are at Bower's Hill; that there were troops of ours on the Nansemond river firing into the Yankee Gunboats and that we had sunk nine out of ten. These ladies report that we have a most decided victory at Charleston. We can get no newspapers.*

*Saturday, April 18, 1863. Fair and mild. Peter, our foreman left during the night for Freedom. Liske who was next in value to Peter, left some time ago but we thought he might return to his work as soon as he recovered his health as he staid at Deep Creek with his wife. We now know that both are gone, all the hired hands except two left with Peter. Our corn is planted with no one to work the crop through. Today the yankees came up from Deep Creek and rebuilt the canal bridge and about five hundred of their cavalry (most of them the same that stopped here on the 13th.) went out to South Mills where they were to meet our troops. About twenty of their number were left at the bridge and we are expecting them to take some of our horses tonight if they can find them. This has been a day of painful excitement with us. We are in a dilemma about taking our negroes and the women and children over the lines. Some of the yankees have sunk our largest lighter {canal boat} by cutting holes in the sides. Mr. Wallace was offered 1000$ for her a short time ago and now she is worthless. We are progressing downwards at a rapid rate.*

*Sunday, April 19, 1863. Fair and pleasant weather. We shall long remember this Sunday. Heavy cannon have been firing all day rapidly in the direction of Nansemond River. Certainly not less than a thousand or fifteen [hundred] projectiles have been doing a work of destruction. We cannot tell what it means but a yankee said today to Mr. Wallace that it was their gun boats firing to keep our soldiers from crossing the Nansemond. We have heard nothing from the troops that went out yesterday to meet our people.*

*Glencoe Diary*, written by Elizabeth Curtis Wallace. Reprinted by permission of the Norfolk County Historical Society.

## Section 2. (B) Great Dismal Swamp Boat Ramp to (C) Dismal Swamp Canal Visitor Information Center - 7 miles, one way. Chesapeake, VA and Camden County, NC

After passing under the bridge at Deep Creek in the City of Chesapeake, Virginia and all the way to Camden County, North Carolina, the Dismal Swamp Canal makes one turn called "The Angle." There are few deviations in the scenery, but the paddler can be on the lookout for the original stone markers noting the canal's miles. See page 49 for a history of these mysterious markers. The Visitor Center is located at Mile 28 on the Intracoastal Waterway (ICW) along the Dismal Swamp Canal in Camden County, NC. Arriving by water, the take-out for this section is at the sandy access spot between a break in the old wooden bulkhead just past the dock at the Dismal Swamp Visitor Center. A short carry through a shaded walk leads to the pavement and the parking lot is a short distance. The amenities at the Visitor Center are a most welcome oasis. Take time to visit the gift shop as it contains a treasure trove of information about the area and nearby attractions.

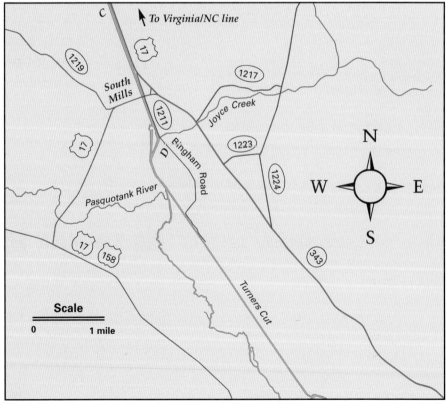

**Map 4:** Dismal Swamp Canal from South Mills to the Pasquotank River        © Vickie Shufer

## Section 3. (C) The Dismal Swamp Canal Visitor Information Center to (D) SR 1211/Joy's Creek Road – $^8/_{10}$ miles. Camden County, NC

Downstream, the take-out point in South Mills is north of the bridge on U.S. Business 17/Main Street. The South Mills Lock is at Mile 32.8 along the Dismal Swamp Canal. The lock allows boats to be raised or lowered about 9 feet. Since all sailboats and motor yachts will require the use of the lock, it is suggested out of courtesy that canoes and kayaks take out before the lock along the east side of the DSC and walk around for passage along the canal. The goal is to get around the locks to SR 1211/Joy's Creek Road, south of the bridge. This is a healthy portage around the locks. If not desiring this work-out, it is possible to pull a vehicle off the road enough to load a canoe or kayak and drive to the south side of the locks. Do not put back in again until south of the steel bulkheaded canal banks. Here, the edges of the bank have been kept free of shrubs and there are several good spots to launch.

### River Highlights

Even though the scenery remains unchanged on this straight stretch of waterway, the plant life does offer some diversity. Red maples are common most of the way intermixed with bald cypress and water tupelo. The shrub layer consists of cyrilla, sweet pepperbush, pawpaws and possum haw. Muscadine grape vines drape across the banks, especially on the west side.

### The Dismal Swamp Nature Trail

The ¼ mile nature trail begins at the northwest corner of the Visitor Center's parking lot at the water's edge and makes a loop through the adjacent forest. Interpretive signs indicate many of the local tree species including sassafras, sweetgum, pignut hickory, red mulberry, black cherry, eastern redcedar, red maple, sycamore, loblolly pine and pin oak.

For more information, contact Dismal Swamp Visitor Center, 2356 Highway 17 North, South Mills, NC 27976, (252) 771-8333 or visit their web site at www.icw.net/dscwelcome.

**DISMAL SWAMP NATURE TRAIL**

**1/4 MILE TRAIL**

*Please Do Not Litter*

*Caution: Beware of Snakes*

*vs*

*vs*

## The "Loki" Educational Exhibit

The "Loki" is a small gasoline-powered locomotive that operated on "tram lines" or temporary narrow gauge rail lines. Diminutive locomotives like this one were used to haul logs out of the Dismal Swamp and other Southern forests.

William Spaur's pleasure boat, "Grace" of Gilmerton Cut, on the Dismal Swamp Canal    *vs*

# *Childhood Memories of Steamboats, Circa 1915-1925*

When the authors asked R.E.B. Stewart, great, great grandson of William Charles Stewart, to relate an old story about the Dismal Swamp Canal, he remembered hearing two female cousins tell of their steamship voyages to Portsmouth. His great, great grandfather was a neighbor of the Wallace family (of Wallaceton along the route of the Dismal Swamp Canal). W.C. Stewart built Beechwood, his family's 1800's plantation home located on Bell Haven Street in Chesapeake within walking distance of the site of the Wallace House, Glencoe. R.E.B.'s family history is interwoven with the history of Norfolk County.

> *Truck boats took the area crops (vegetables grown along the east side of the canal) to the farmers' markets in Norfolk and Portsmouth. Some truck crops were transferred to other vessels for shipment to Richmond, Washington, or Baltimore. Vegetables were also sent to Elizabeth City.*
>
> *The truck boats also carried passengers. My cousins, who were sisters, recalled getting up very early each Saturday to catch the boat at West's Landing. Upon landing in Portsmouth, they went to Miss Agnes Earnest's home for piano lessons. Following piano, they had lunch and a 'dope' at Betty Taylor's Candy Kitchen on King Street (near the current library). 'Dope' came from the rumor that the druggist inventor of our most popular soft drink used cocaine in his original formula.*
>
> *After a downtown shopping tour and a trip to the library, it was time to catch the truck boat back to West's Landing where a buggy was waiting to take them home. The truck boat was not only vital to commerce, it provided a passage for many of the citizens of south Norfolk County.*
>
> – Stewart, R.E.B. Unpublished manuscript, 2002.

*A trip through its canals is a wonderful summer day's experience, with overhanging gum and cypress and red maple branches meeting the intertwining and bald knees of the cypress trunks rising fantastically to the bodies of great trees.*

– Floyd McKnight, 1959

# Part Three

# The Great Dismal Swamp and Lake Drummond

*It is the source of no less than 5 Several Rivers which discharge themselves Southward into Albemarle Sound ...*

*— William Byrd, 1728*

# The Great Dismal Swamp and Lake Drummond

The Great Dismal Swamp begins on the eastern side of a ridge called the Nansemond or Suffolk Escarpment, the edge of an ancient ocean. Surveyed in colonial days at over 2,000 square miles, today it is protected as over 111,000 acres of the Great Dismal Swamp National Wildlife Refuge. Today the world's largest stands of Atlantic White-cedar can be found here as well as five major forest types.

In the heart of the swamp is Lake Drummond, a natural lake that is 3,100 acres in extent, but shallow enough that most professional basketball players could wade across and not get their hair wet. The lake can be visited along designated routes by hiking, bicycling or boating into the swamp.

## Location

The Great Dismal Swamp is located forty percent in southeastern Virginia and sixty percent in northeastern North Carolina. The western boundary is represented by a sand ridge called the Suffolk Escarpment. The Dismal Swamp Canal, parallel to U.S. 17 in Chesapeake, Virginia and Camden County, North Carolina, marks the current eastern boundary.

## Access Site

A. **Great Dismal Swamp Boat Ramp**

> *...the most beautiful and magnificent feature of the region...*
> – Edmund Ruffin, 1837

Lake Drummond in the Great Dismal Swamp                    *Photo by Paul Shufer*

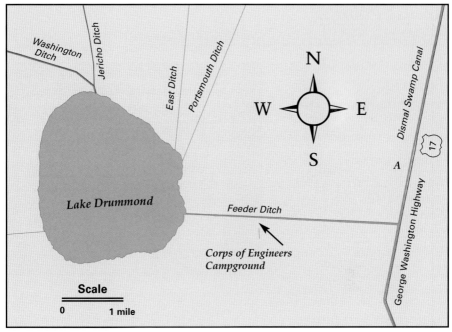

**Map 5:** The Great Dismal Swamp/Lake Drummond                    © Vickie Shufer

The name, Great Dismal Swamp, and the place have a truly magical feel. There are ghost stories, poems, American Indian legends, and local tall tales about it. Today most travelers see nothing more of the Great Dismal Swamp than the view from a car speeding along U.S. 17 in Chesapeake, Virginia or Camden County, North Carolina. Parallel to this automobile route, which was formerly a stagecoach road, is the Dismal Swamp Canal, the oldest continuously operating canal in the Western Hemisphere. The traveler may be unaware of the historical significance of the area to American Indians, colonial Americans in peace and war, runaway slaves, the armies of the Union and Confederacy, the economic advantages to the suppliers and shippers of products north and south, and today's pleasure boaters. For more information on The Dismal Swamp Canal, see p. 32 .

---

## When is a Swamp Not a Swamp?

A swamp is a wet forested area that is flooded at least once during a growing season. While this may have been true at one time in the Dismal Swamp, the ditching that has taken place has drained much of the land, especially outside the refuge, reducing the amount of swamp land from what it once was. Wet areas with nonwoody vegetation are marshes and the spongy areas where peat has developed are bogs.

---

# Access Point
## (A) Great Dismal Swamp Boat Ramp

While there are 51 major ditches with over 196 miles of ditch work (Trout, 1998) in the Great Dismal Swamp National Wildlife Refuge, currently there is only one public canoe/kayak trail into Lake Drummond. This is the Feeder Ditch perpendicular to the Dismal Swamp Canal that parallels U.S. Route 17/George Washington Highway.

*Photo by George Ramsey*

*Directions*: From I-64 take Dominion Blvd, SR 104 west to U.S. 17/George Washington Highway and go south approximately 14 miles. The Great Dismal Swamp Boat Ramp is on the west side of U.S. 17 near the intersection of West Ballahack Road, in Chesapeake, Virginia. This is a paved ramp with plenty of parking. The no-fee public launch site contains no restroom facilities.

*Facilities*: Where the Feeder Ditch meets the spillway, a small railway, when operating, helps transport boats from the southern side of the Feeder Ditch to the western side of the spillway. There is no charge for this service. The camping facilities are described below.

*Camping*: One of the best kept secrets about the Dismal Swamp is the tent camping available free of charge at the U.S. Army Corps of Engineers Campground. Located near the spillway at the western end of the Feeder Ditch, the campground has restrooms and two large screened areas for eating or meeting, and eight picnic tables. There is no potable water on site but water is available for non-drinking uses. Reservations are not taken, as this is a first-come-first-serve area. Call (757) 421-7401 for additional information.

*Ownership*: The U.S. Army Corps of Engineers maintains the Dismal Swamp Canal, the Feeder Ditch, the dam at the spillway, the campground, the railway, and the camping area. The Great Dismal Swamp National Wildlife Refuge is managed by the U.S. Fish and Wildlife Service of the Department of the Interior.

# Prehistoric Swamp

Today the ocean is about thirty miles from the Dismal Swamp, but that has not always been the case. The Suffolk Escarpment is a Pleistocene-era (1.6 million years ago) seashore marking the western edge of the Great Dismal Swamp. Ocean levels have risen and fallen over the years. The most recent occurred around 14,000 years ago, during an interruption in the last Ice Age. As the glaciers readvanced, the ocean waters receded as water was taken up in the ice sheets. A boreal pine-spruce forest developed on the ridges as the climate at that time was short cool summers and long cold winters, necessary conditions for the formation of peat.

It is believed that hunters and their families first arrived here more than 12,000 years ago, probably following herds of mammoths, mastodons and bison, which they used for food and clothing. As the ice age came to a close and the climate became warmer, the variety and abundance of plant and animal life enabled the establishment of seasonal camps. About 3,000 years ago, the Indians moved from the forested swamp and established villages along rivers and waterways, returning to the swamp for short-term hunting (Lecture, Old Dominion University, Norfolk, VA, 1976).

# Connecting To The Past

*While attending a Great Dismal Swamp Archaeology class, I was involved in a dig on White Marsh Road along the Suffolk Scarp (Escarpment). We spent two days working at a site known to be near other ancient encampment sites. As a first-timer, I had visions of unearthing arrowheads, pottery shards and stone tools. We were having no luck finding anything until we hit a layer of soil containing bits of charcoal. We carefully excavated what had been a campfire, exposing the fire circle and a bit beyond. Ed Bottoms, our instructor, pointed out bits of charred wood that were outside the circle indicating the direction the wind had been blowing on a cool evening, maybe a thousand or more years ago. Standing over the small charred area, it was possible to see the path where someone had swept a hand or more likely a foot across the last of the coals. Looking at the scattered charcoal, it reminded me of doing exactly the same thing the last time I had gone camping. What a connected feeling to the past to see where a concerned person of so very long ago had double-checked to make sure the fire was completely out and it was safe to leave and move on.*

*– Lillie's Field Notes, November 1, 1975*

# Paddling Sections

## Section 1. (A) Great Dismal Swamp Boat Ramp to Dismal Swamp Feeder Ditch – ¾ mile.

The Dismal Swamp Canal is an alternate route of the Atlantic Intracoastal Waterway and may have heavy boat traffic. This is a popular route for spring and fall yachtsmen going north or south. Paddlers need to turn south out of the boat launch site into the canal. After ¾ of a mile, at what has been known as Arbuckle Landing, turn west into the Feeder Ditch. Go almost 3 miles to the U.S. Army Corps of Engineers spillway where it is necessary to portage and paddle another half-mile on the canal that leads straight, literally, to Lake Drummond.

## River Highlights

This swamp is different from most southern swamps in that it is not flat. Water flows from this gently sloping basin from its highest points in the northwest to the southeast. The drop however is slight, only 3 meters over the entire expanse of its current 15 kilometer expanse (Terwilliger, 2000).

Although the canal itself is straight and the scenery doesn't seem to change, the plant life along the banks is diverse and does change. The east side is shaded with water tupelo trees along the banks and red maple and sweetgum on higher ground. Numerous shrubs grow in the understory.

### Muscadine Grapes

Covering the west bank of the Dismal Swamp Canal is a thick growth of vines. Upon closer inspection, one will notice that it is almost entirely muscadine grape. These are the native ancestors of the cultivated muscadine and produce an abundance of grapes that ripen in the fall.

## Bears in the Dismal Swamp

An interesting map drawn by Augustin Herrman in 1670 and published in 1673 bears the inscription, "The land between the James River and Roanoke River is for the most parts Low Suncken Swampy Land not well passable but with great difficulty. And therein harbours Tygers, Bears and other Devouringe Creatures" (Brown, 1981). While "Tygers" have not been seen (although large bobcats have), bears have long been at home in the Dismal Swamp. Over ninety years after Mr. Herrman's narrative, in 1763, a land patent was recorded for Nansemond County as "Beg. in the great Juniper Sw., up the E side of the Mill br., through the great Beargarden..." (Hudgins, 1999). One wonders if the "Beargarden" was a reference to an area frequented by bears.

In 1994 and again in 2001, it was estimated that the Dismal Swamp was home to 350 black bears, the largest concentration on the east coast. The usually docile bears can grow to 300 pounds or more with an average life span of 15 to 30 years. The largest recorded bear ever killed in eastern Virginia was near Whaleyville, Virginia to the west of the Dismal Swamp. It was seven feet tall and weighed 740 pounds. He was shot during a bear hunt in December of 2000 (Bertie-Camp, 2001). While largely vegetarian, black bears are opportunists and will eat insects, meat, fish and carrion. The young males, typically at about age two, start to roam away from their family unit, sometimes wandering as far as 50 miles (Mather, 1994).

While this roaming instinct was not a concern hundreds of years ago, for the bears of the 21st century, it means trouble. This traveling pattern has meant death for many of the swamp's bears. On May 10, 1994, it was reported that nine bears had been hit by cars on local roads over a period of one and a half years (Daniel, 1994). In 2003, more than 20 bears were killed by vehicles in Suffolk and Chesapeake.

The Great Dismal Swamp National Wildlife Refuge, although larger

 in land area than Portsmouth and Norfolk combined, appears not to be large enough to contain the bears' wanderings. The pre-colonial swamp comprised one to two million acres of land. Currently, the acreage is diminished to about 150,000 acres (Daniel, 1994). The federal protection the bears enjoy inside the refuge boundaries

Black Bear　　　*Photo by Pat Cuffee*

cannot save them as they venture into the ever-increasing developments and highways in the area. With loss of habitat and wilderness travel routes, the largest mammal in Virginia faces an uncertain future. There is a bright spot in the forecast though. To try to eliminate some of the deadly interaction between bears and other wildlife with motorized vehicles, at least one wildlife underpass has been planned by the Virginia Department of Transportation as U.S. 17 is widened.

Black Bear                                    *Photo by Pat Cuffee*

## *Section 2. Dismal Swamp Feeder Ditch to Spillway – 3 miles, one way.*

The plant life changes somewhat when you reach the feeder ditch. Instead of muscadine grapes, fruit-bearing trees and shrubs line the banks on both sides, providing a refreshing nibble in the hot summer months.

One of the most productive is the black cherry. A small tree, the branches hang over the water. The berries are small, about one-fourth inch in diameter and turn reddish-black when ripe. When mashed, they leave a purplish stain.

Randomly scattered along the banks are blackberry bushes with sweet and juicy fruits. The branches are armed with sharp thorns. The abundance of fruit trees and shrubs, together with a healthy insect population, makes this area a hot spot for birdwatching. Both cherries and blackberries are among favorite summer foods for black bears.

Blackberries   *Photo by Pat Cuffee*

68

# Section 3. Spillway to Lake Drummond – ½ mile

To paddle into the almost circular lake feels like a trip back in time. All of the old lake houses are gone and only a couple of docks remain, one at Washington Ditch. Lake Drummond is the largest one of only two natural lakes in the state of Virginia, the other being Mountain Lake near Blacksburg (not to be confused with Smith Mountain Lake near Roanoke, Virginia). Covering more than 3,000 acres, it's about 2½ miles wide by 3 miles long.

## River Highlights

Bald cypress trees ring the lake with their knees forming a natural border as one enters the lake from the entrance canal off the Feeder Ditch. The lake bottom has a layer of sand over a layer of peat or mud as well as a lot of downed trees that are not visible due to the cola-dark tannin water.

Paddling north along the edge of the lake from the feeder ditch for less than a mile will bring you to Portsmouth Ditch. Although the ditch is not navigable, it is possible to come ashore, stretch your legs, and get a feeling of being in the swamp. Be aware, however, that all three poisonous snakes of Virginia, the copperhead, canebrake rattlesnake and cottonmouth, live here in the swamp and their color patterns make them almost impossible to see unless they move.

Copperhead        *Photo by Pat Cuffee*

## Juniper Water

The color of the water in the lake and the canals is one of the first things about which a newcomer comments. The water is so dark that a blind species of fish lives there (*Chologaster cornuta*). This fish is commonly referred to as the "Swamp Fish." Tannins from several types of vegetation color the water and give it a fairly low pH. Once a valuable commodity, this acid rich water was barreled and sent across the Atlantic on sailing ships in the 1800s. The acidic brew was resistant to bacterial growth and thus safely used as drinking water on long sea voyages. It is part of the folklore of the area that Blackbeard purchased water from Lake Drummond for his pirate crew. It is also reported that Commodore Perry carried Dismal Swamp water on his voyage to Japan. Today we cannot recommend drinking the water from the canals or the lake due to agricultural activity in the surrounding area.

## Section 4.  Feeder Ditch to Washington Ditch – less than 2½ miles.

To the north and west from Portsmouth Ditch is Washington Ditch. On a calm day, one can set a compass at 340° WNW and paddle north and west across the lake to Washington Ditch. Here one can get out, take a walk along the ditches to the intersection of Washington and Jericho Ditch, or beyond, and have a snack on the deck overlooking the lake.

### Lake Origins

There are several speculations about the origin of Lake Drummond. One is of a prehistoric meteorite creating a "Carolina Bay." The *Aeromagnetic Map of Virginia* shows a magnetic anomaly in the swamp near Lake Drummond and compasses don't always work. Even George Washington almost missed the lake when Washington Ditch was dug.

Another theory is that it was formed by a peat fire. When dry, peat burns very slowly and can spread underground, sometimes burning for years before it is put out, often by a long period of rain. This theory is supported by an Indian legend of a huge firebird with a burning nest in the middle of the swamp.

### Fishing

Fishing is permitted in the lake with a freshwater license. However, due to the acidity of the dark, tannic water and because light doesn't penetrate easily, the fish population is limited. The surface water heats up in the summer and its ability to hold oxygen is not very great, reducing the algae or other photosynthetic plants. Fish that can survive here include catfish, perch, sunfish, bluegill, pumpkinseed, flier, bass and crappie.

---

### *Helpful Wetlands Plant*

*At lunchtime our group of three kayaks and five canoes pulled up to the shoreline near the campground. As we settled into our seats near the spillway, Vickie bounded away into the woods and came back with some leaves for us. "I thought you might want to wash your hands. Sweet pepperbush, poor man's soap!" We all "washed" our hands in the lather produced by the helpful leaves (see p. 96).*

*– Lillie's Journal Notes*
*October 27, 1998*

---

## Otter Tales

We were with a group of paddlers, walking along the edge of Washington Ditch when someone noticed bubbles on the surface of the water. We stopped and watched. Soon a nose emerged, took a look at the group, and dove back under, leaving behind a circle of bubbles. A few seconds later, the head popped up again, this time a little farther

River Otter          *Photo by Pat Cuffee*

down. We followed. Then we noticed the otter was keeping our pace, surfacing, then diving under and stayed with us until we got almost back to our boats.

Otters are playful animals and like to slide down mud banks into the water. Bare, slick spots on the bank are indicators that otters are nearby. A fishy smell can also be linked to otters since fish is a big part of their diet.

Beaver          *Photo by Pat Cuffee*

## Bobcats

A medium-sized cat, bobcats are natural predators in the swamp. They hunt mostly at night and prey on rabbits, squirrels, turkey, rodents and deer (as carrion). They prefer thick, second growth forests where there are clearings, but are occasionally seen stalking prey along the dirt roads within the refuge.

## Beavers

The beaver is the largest rodent in North America and weighs from 26 to 90 pounds. Even though you don't always see the beaver, you can look for signs of where they have been. They build dams from felled trees, often creating new ponds behind the dam.

Bobcat          *Photo by Pat Cuffee*

## Hunting Tradition

Collection of Lillie Gilbert

One of the interesting habits of the hunters in the Dismal Swamp involved the initiation of the hunter bagging his/her first deer in the swamp. If we can imagine the hunting lodges of long past surrounding Lake Drummond, a similarity among them would be the collection of multi-colored tattered rags nailed to the "cabins." The local tradition was to cut (or rip) a piece of the hunter's shirt that was worn during the first kill of a deer within the swamp's boundaries. The cloth strips were all about 4-5" long by a couple of inches wide, so there was some uniformity of this quirky habit. These were then nailed to the door of the lakeside dwelling in which the hunter was staying. Some of the "lucky lodges" had many, many colorful scraps flapping in the breeze (Gammon, 2002). Today very little is left along the lake's edge to remind the paddler of the old cabins.

### White-tail Deer/Hunting

White-tail deer are frequently spotted in the Dismal Swamp along the forest edges, or more frequently, retreating into the swamp, waving their tails to alert other deer of danger. There is a deer hunt in the fall, so if you are planning a trip at that time of year, be sure to check with the Great Dismal Swamp National Wildlife Refuge headquarters at 757-986-3705 for dates and times.

White-tail Deer                    Photo by Pat Cuffee

*Deer are common, but hard to get. In the fall hunters run them into the lake and catch them with dogs.*

– A.K. Fisher, 1895

## A Spooky Experience on Lake Drummond

One particularly interesting experience at the lake occurred several years ago. While canoeing on the lake on a very still night, we heard voices. Our group knew that we were not only the lone campers at the campground, but we were absolutely certain that we were the only paddlers on the dark lake. The situation was even stranger when we realized that the voices were ours. Every word, every sound uttered by the canoeists was repeated from the shoreline.

Our eerie experience turned out to be not as supernatural as natural. It appears that at a certain point on the circular lake, the treed shoreline acts as a parabolic sound reflector; our voices were echoed. What a fascinating place!

Night paddling is no longer allowed on the lake, but the effect can occur in daylight. Try it the next time you paddle into this ever-amazing lake.

*... half a mile into the Dismal. the skirts of it were thinly planted with Dwarf Reeds and Gall-Bushes, but when we got into the Dismal itself, we found the Reeds grew there much taller and closer, and, to mend the matter was so interlac'd with bamo-briars, that there was no scuffling thro' them without the help of Pioneers. At the same time, we found the Ground moist and trembling under our feet like a Quagmire, insomuch that it was an easy Matter to run a Ten-Foot-Pole up to the Head in it, without exerting any uncommon Strength to do it.*

– William Byrd, 1728

Greenbrier Leaf

## Peat Beds

One of the unique features of the Great Dismal Swamp is the layer of peat, in some places more than fourteen feet thick, that is found throughout the swamp. If you scoop up a handful of peat and look at it up close, you will see leaf veins and other partially decomposed plant material. Peat develops in areas that have long cold winters and short, cool summers with sufficient moisture and trees with acidic litter. Once peat has established itself, the acidity inhibits the breakdown of plant material and the peat beds continue to grow. An experiment to try is to find a straight stick and see how far you can push it into the ground.

"George Washington at Lake Drummond," from Irving's Life of Washington, 1859.

## Drummonds Pond and Washington Ditch

The lake we know as Lake Drummond was called "Drummonds Pond" at least by 1759. Virginia Land Patent Book 33, bearing the recorded notes of July 4, 1759, states that Mills Riddick paid 5 Shillings for "25 acs. Nansemond Co. on the N side of Drummonds Pond in the Desert."

In the early 1760's Norfolk County's Gershom Nimmo was employed by George Washington and Fielding Lewis to survey part of the Dismal Swamp. His 1763 map shows a "causeway" going from the road on the west side of the Dismal almost to the lake. Later, a 12-foot wide, 5-mile long transport ditch was dug which still bears the name, "Washington Ditch." The earliest found written reference to this first ditch is a Virginia Gazette advertisement of 1772 in which the Riddick estate of 75 acres is listed as "joining the great ditch in the Dismal Swamp, which abounds with great plenty of Cypress timber" (Brown, 1970). Although Washington has been credited with surveying Washington Ditch and the Dismal Swamp Canal, it may be that Gershom Nimmo surveyed the area in addition to his work on other parts of the swamp (Whichard, 1959). The surveyor's name will be familiar to Tidewater Virginia readers because of Nimmo Church and Nimmo Parkway in Virginia Beach, Virginia. Gershom Nimmo was brother to William Nimmo whose wife, Anne, donated the land upon which Nimmo Church was built in 1791.

# A Short History of the Great Dismal Swamp

We do not know the American Indians' name for this area. By 1650 there were relatively few natives left near the Dismal Swamp. The early English settlers first referred to this land as "the Desert" (meaning "an inhospitable place") and deeds or patents referring to the Desert are recorded as early as 1702 (Nugent, 1979). Desert Road exists in Suffolk today. The first recorded land purchase bearing the descriptive name "Dismal" occurs in 1738 when for one pound and 5 shillings, Doctor William Happer purchased "250 acs. of Low Sunken L. in Norf. Co.on the NW side of the North West Riv. & known by the Name of the Dismal, by the Cypress Sw., along the Light Sw." (Hudgins, 1979).

The lake in the center of the Great Dismal Swamp is thought to be named for a hunter, a Mister Drummond, who discovered it after he got lost in the swamp. It has also been thought to have been named for William Drummond (1663-1667), the first governor of North Carolina, but historical sources no longer support this claim (Levy, 2001).

As described in an early diary, the "Virginia Road" led travelers from the Nansemond River along the higher ground of the western edge of the Great Dismal Swamp into Carolina. Founder of the Society of Friends, Quaker George Fox in October of 1672 traveled by canoe from Norfolk to the Nansemond River and then by horseback along the trail-like road. He described the "Road" as having notches chopped in tree trunks to guide the way. The area was jungle-like and probably frightening to early travelers. Fox wrote that the trip along the Road took two days by horseback from the Nansemond River to Bennetts Creek and his group was "commonly wet to the Knees... and lay abroad a-Nights in the Woods by a Fire" (Snell, 1974).

William Byrd II, while surveying the dividing line between Virginia and North Carolina in 1728, was not too impressed with the swamp. He wrote in a letter that "No human creature had ever ventured over this dreadful place before ..." (Mitchell, Pague and Schwab, 2001). George Washington, however, had a

Draining Land

*Collection of Lillie Gilbert*

*Collection of Lillie Gilbert*

different perception of the swamp. He saw it as a "glorious paradise abounding in wild fowl and game" (Handley, 2001) and wanted to drain it and farm it. The soil turned out to be too acidic for farming, so instead he turned to logging. In 1763, the company known as "Adventurers for Draining the Great Dismal Swamp" began the ditching and logging operation. Washington and fellow "Adventurers" William and Thomas Nelson, Robert Burwell, Washington's brother-in-law Fielding Lewis, Robert Tucker, Jr. of Norfolk, Thomas Walker, William Waters, John Symes and Samuel Gist made up the group. Washington and five of the associates are said to have acquired 40,000 acres of timberland said to have "the finest cypress, juniper and other

Timber cutters going into the swamp

lofty wood" (Brown, 1970). Commercial activity has continued by various groups until 1976 with the entire swamp having been logged at least once. With the years of draining and logging, the swamp has changed drastically since Washington circumnavigated it on horseback in May of 1763 (Simpson, 1990). Residential, agricultural and commercial development has reduced the size of the swamp to a fraction of its original size and biodiversity has suffered. The cypress-tupelo and Atlantic white-cedar forests that dominated the swamp in colonial days have mostly been replaced by red maple, sweetgum and tulip poplar.

**DISMAL TOWN**

WASHINGTON AND COMPANY USED THIS SPOT AS THEIR DISMAL SWAMP HEAD-QUARTERS. THE TOWN WAS BUILT PRIOR TO THE NIMMO SURVEY OF 1763 ON RIDDICK 402 ACRE PATENT.

vs

In October, 1969, a group of private citizens, scholars, scientists, and members of non-profit conservation organizations attended a meeting sponsored by the Virginia Division of the Izaak Walton League in Suffolk, Virginia. A Dismal Swamp Preservation Committee was formed and for several years, various individuals and groups made their thoughts known concerning the need to preserve the Dismal Swamp. Private industry officials and legislators were made aware of the plight of the swamp. The late Mr. Alvah Carter Duke is credited with much of the energy dedicated to the cause of saving the Dismal Swamp. A grant of 22,500 hectares, (over 55,000 acres) by the Union Camp Corporation set the stage and President Gerald Ford, on August 30, 1974, signed into law the bill to establish the Great Dismal Swamp National Wildlife Refuge (Ashley, 2000). The land was transferred from the Union Camp Corporation to the Nature Conservancy and finally to the Secretary of the Interior. The Refuge has been managed since then by the Northeast Region of the U.S. Fish and Wildlife Service.

## *The Great Dismal Swamp National Wildlife Refuge*

The Great Dismal Swamp National Wildlife Refuge is one of more than 500 refuges managed by the U.S. Fish and Wildlife Service. Maintaining the water resources with water control structures, restoring the native plant communities through forest management activities and providing the required habitat for wildlife are essential to the swamp ecosystem.

The Refuge headquarters is located at 3100 Desert Road, Suffolk, Virginia, with restrooms and information available for visitors from Monday to Friday, 8:00-3:30. The Refuge trails are open daily from ½ hour before sunrise to ½ hour after sunset for nature study, photography, hiking, biking, boating and sight-seeing. Hurricane Isabel did incredible damage to the swamp and its trails in September, 2003. Call the Refuge at 757-986-3705 for updates. The dirt road that parallels the historic Washington Ditch is currently open and extends to Lake Drummond. It is 4½ miles long and excellent for bicycling. At the end is a dock overlooking the lake and a great spot for a picnic.

The trail at Washington Ditch is a watchable wildlife site on the

Virginia Birding and Wildlife Trail. For more information on this coastal phase of the trail, go to www.dgif.state.va.us.

*Directions*

To reach the western side of the Great Dismal Swamp, take I-64 East toward Bower's Hill in Suffolk. Follow the signs for U.S. 13, 58, 460 and take the exit for Downtown Suffolk. Go almost one mile and make a left on Route 337/Washington Street. Follow this about 2¼ miles to the intersection of Route 642/White Marsh Road and go south (left). The entrance to Jericho Lane is about 1¾ miles on the left. For Washington Ditch, continue south approximately 6 miles and look for the refuge sign on the east (left) side of the road. A gravel road will lead to the parking area which is a little over one mile from the turn-off. To reach the headquarters, continue south from Washington Ditch on Route 642/White Marsh Road about 1 mile to the stop sign at the intersection of Desert Road. Turn east (left) on Desert Road and go almost 2 miles. Look for the Refuge signs; the entrance is on the left. Follow the road to the parking area.

For more information and a free brochure, contact Great Dismal Swamp National Wildlife Refuge, 3100 Desert Road, Suffolk, VA 23434, (757) 986-3705.

## Dismal Swamp State Park

North Carolina is beginning to establish a new state park in the Camden County portion of the Dismal Swamp. The park will be open to public use on its 14,700 acre site. A showpiece of the park will be the visitor's center encompassing 6,500 square feet to be located next to the existing Dismal Swamp Canal Visitor Information Center on U.S. 17. The area has long needed an interpretive center and this long awaited project already has $2.4 million allocated by the Parks and Recreation Authority from its Trust Fund. Earlier funds were allocated for the design process.

The park will be located across the Dismal Swamp Canal on the west side, just three miles from the NC/VA state line. To access the new park, visitors will walk across an 80' floating bridge on the canal. Henry Stokes, a veteran of North Carolina's park system since 1980, will be its first superintendent. He is a canoeist, enjoying whitewater as well as flatwater; certified in environmental education as well as advanced law enforcement; and is trained in search and rescue. The authors welcome the new park and its well-qualified superintendent in the newest chapter of the Great Dismal Swamp. For information call (252) 482-7455.

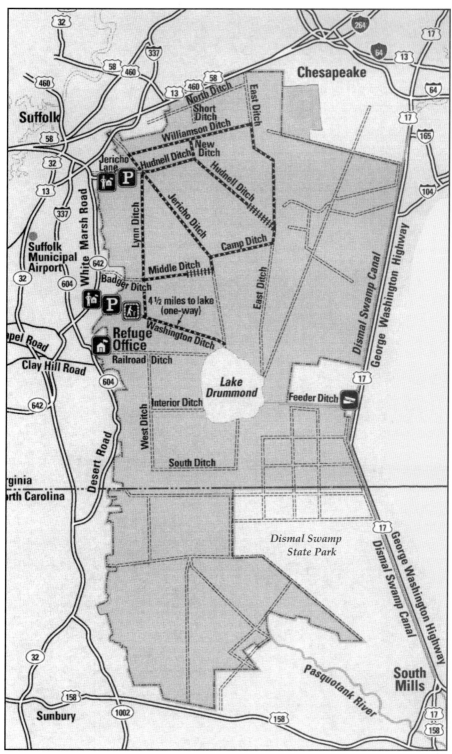

*Map courtesy of U.S. Fish & Wildlife Service*

# Suffolk and Chesapeake –
# Homes to the Great Dismal Swamp in Virginia

**Suffolk, Virginia,** when it merged with Nansemond County in 1974, created one of the most extensive cities in the United States and, with 430 square miles, became the largest city in Virginia. Part of the Great Dismal Swamp is within its city limits. Trading by the early English settlers with the Nansemond Indians may date as far back as 1608. The Suffolk community was permanently settled in 1720, chartered in 1742, and was named for Suffolk, England. Its location along the Nansemond and James Rivers made it the perfect starting point for a trip southward into Carolina from Virginia. During colonial times, there were only two roads heading south. One was from Suffolk on the western side of the Dismal Swamp. This road was originally an animal migration route, later an Indian trail (today's White Marsh Road). The other road was the old stage road paralleling the Dismal Swamp Canal leading from Norfolk through present-day Chesapeake, Virginia to Elizabeth City, North Carolina, built after the establishment of the Dismal Swamp Canal. The part of the stage road in North Carolina was built on the old Indian trail (now part of NC Route 34 and NC Route 343).

When visiting Suffolk today, be sure to see the exhibits at the city's Visitor Center located in the **Seaboard Airline Passenger Station** built in 1885, located at 326 North Main Street, Suffolk, Virginia 23434. Across the street at 321 North Main Street is the recently restored **Prentis House**, circa 1800, which may be the oldest standing building in Suffolk. Originally designed to be a manor house, it now serves as Suffolk's **Division of Tourism** offices and the Visitor Information Center, (757) 923-3880. Nearby are many historic homes and shops in Suffolk's Historic District located between Constant's Wharf on North Main Street to Washington Street including Bank and Pinner Streets. **Riddick's Folly**, built in 1837 is a twenty-room Greek Revival style home that is now a museum and cultural center located at 510 North Main Street. Most homes from the 1700's no longer exist as the town was captured and burned by the British in 1779 during the Revolutionary War. Suffolk was occupied during the Civil War by Union Troops. For more information on Suffolk, contact www.suffolk.va.us.

**Chesapeake, Virginia,** which derives its name from the great Bay, is not contiguous with the Chesapeake Bay at all. It is not land-locked because of its notable creeks and rivers which connect it to the

Chesapeake Bay and the world via the Western Branch of the Elizabeth River, the Southern Branch of the Elizabeth River, the North Landing River, and Pocaty River. Its most well-known waterways include most of Lake Drummond in the Great Dismal Swamp, the Albemarle and Chesapeake Canal, and the Dismal Swamp Canal. Part of the North Landing River Natural Area Preserve, referred to by The Nature Conservancy as "one of Virginia's last great places," is within Chesapeake's city limits. The Northwest River, with its original headwaters in the Dismal Swamp is located mostly in Chesapeake and drains to the southeast emptying into Currituck Sound in North Carolina. Deep Creek Lock Park and Northwest River Park are city parks not to be missed. Read more about them on pages 34 and 108.

The City of Chesapeake was formed in 1963 when the city of South Norfolk and Norfolk County consolidated, forming a city of 353 square miles. Chesapeake is currently the second largest city in the state of Virginia in land area. For more information, contact www.chesapeake.va.us.

## *Future of the Great Dismal Swamp*

The future of the Great Dismal Swamp, its ecology, its animal and plant inhabitants is uncertain as development edges closer and closer. No one says it better than the late Alvah Duke, historian and guide in his essay, I believe, part of which is reprinted below. By reading this essay, the reader can appreciate the beliefs and emotions of one man who made the study, appreciation and saving of the Great Dismal Swamp his life's purpose.

> *The Dismal is the last desperate retreat in an expansive area for the wildlife that seeks sanctuary within its heartland. Here the remaining species kindred to the region will survive, or forever become extinct.*
>
> *Here and here alone, the forces of nature conspired and produced a water whose natural purity has remained unmatched throughout all the annals of time. Here the God of Nature created an eternal spring of amber elixir that repels bacterial attack, being always fresh and pure.*
>
> *The Great Dismal is a once-in-an-earth-time miracle, a fresh-water oasis in a salt-water province, precariously upon a shelf overlooking the sea. Thus the Dismal IS vulnerable. Its elevated position renders it defenseless. It CAN be drained. It IS being drained.*
>
> *And... once destroyed, all the remorseful tears, all the pillars of gold, and all the puny efforts of man can NEVER recreate, imitate, or replace the magnificence of the Great Dismal* (Duke, 1975).

# Part Four

## Northwest River

# Northwest River

The Northwest River drains eastward from the Great Dismal Swamp, beginning in Chesapeake, Virginia and is joined by Indian Creek and Smith Creek in Chesapeake before heading almost due south to the North Carolina line. After leaving Virginia, the Northwest is fed by small-unnamed creeks and by Shingle Landing Creek (also known as Moyock Run or Moyock Creek). Its total navigable length is about 12 miles.

As a paddling river, the Northwest has a lot to offer, from short to long, day or overnight trips. Because the river flows gently from west to east, we will be discussing the Northwest from this direction, which is also from its narrowest to its widest point. The river widens as it travels westward to the bridges on Route 168. After about seven more miles, the Northwest joins Tulls Bay and drains into Currituck Sound in North Carolina. It is from the Currituck Sound that the Northwest River sometimes receives a salty mix to its tannic waters.

## Location

The Northwest River is located in southeastern Virginia in Chesapeake and northeastern North Carolina in Currituck County. It drains eastward from the Great Dismal Swamp into Tulls Bay and joins with the North Landing River in Currituck Sound.

## Access Points

A. **Bunch Walnuts Road Bridge**

B. **Little Arrow Store**

C. **Route 168/Battlefield Boulevard - Bob's Fishing Hole Marina**

D. **Indian Creek Road Bridge**

E. **Smith Creek**

F. **Shingle Landing Creek**

*Ownership:* Besides private ownership of land along the river, 763 acres are owned by the City of Chesapeake (Northwest River Park), The Nature Conservancy and the Virginia Department of Conservation and Recreation as the Northwest River Natural Area Preserve (2,716 acres), and the North Carolina Wildlife Resources Commission as North Carolina Game Lands and North Carolina Bear Preserve.

*If there is magic on this planet, it is contained in water.*

– Loren Eiseley

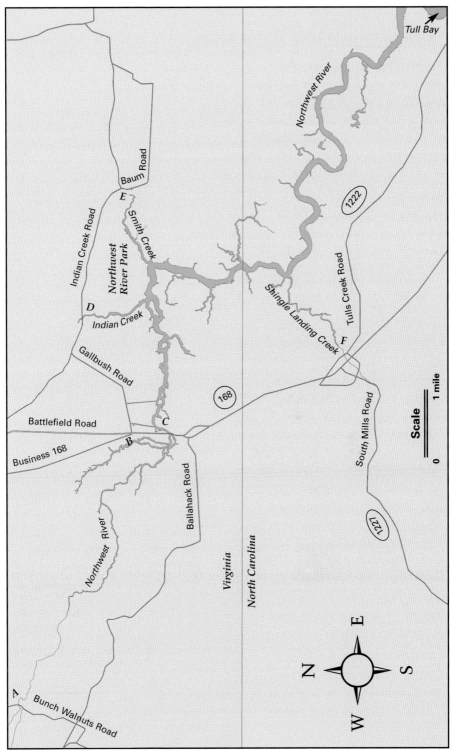

**Map 6:** Northwest River and tributaries

85

© Vickie Shufer

# Access Points

## (A) Bunch Walnuts Road Bridge

*Directions:* From Chesapeake, Virginia drive south on Route 168/Battlefield Boulevard and cross over the Northwest River Bridge. In less than a mile turn west on Old Battlefield Boulevard. From North Carolina, take Route 168 north and cross the NC/VA state line. Just less than a mile, Old Battlefield Boulevard will be the first turn to the west. Follow the road to the corner of Old Battlefield Boulevard and Ballahack Road and turn west. Follow Ballahack west for about 6 miles and turn north at Bunch Walnuts Road. The access is either side of the arched wooden bridge. It is easiest to launch a canoe or kayak from the northwest side, but occasionally high water prohibits this. Parking on the west side will accommodate 2-3 cars.

---

### A Most Special Bridge

Chesapeake, Virginia can be very proud of its unique bridge on a road with a unique name, Bunch Walnuts Road. This gently arched bridge of bent pine and weathered steel is the only one of its kind in the Hampton Roads area. When the old bridge at Bunch Walnuts Road was scheduled for replacement, the Federal Highway Administration had grant money available for "Timber Bridge Construction" projects. Under this program, Chesapeake was able to obtain about half of the money needed for the construction budget. Kevin Lundgren, P.E., of the Chesapeake Department of Public Works was the project engineer and designer of the unusual structure. The pine was supplied by Structural Wood Systems of Greenville, Alabama who shipped the bent wood components of the prefabricated bridge. The T.A. Loving Company of Goldsboro, North Carolina constructed the bridge beginning in August, 1995 with a completion date of March, 1996 (Lundgren, 2001). The location is perfect for this rustic look which adds quite a bit of charm to the river trip.

*Photo by Joe Gilbert*

**Note:** The headwaters of the Northwest River upstream of Bunch Walnuts Road contains extensive swamp forest, other forested wetlands, and upland areas, and forms a very ecologically valuable habitat linkage with the Dismal Swamp. The Nature conservancy has several large holdings in this area, including a 300+ acre tract donated by Andy Griffith. Also included in this area are several compensatory wetland mitigation sites, which comprise nearly 1000 acres of preserved and restored forested wetlands. However, because of often ill-defined channel, beaver activity, the generally swampy nature of much of the area, poor access, and private property concerns, the authors do not recommend paddling in the areas upstream of Bunch Walnuts Road.

## (B) Little Arrow Store

*Directions:* From Route 168/ Battlefield Boulevard, turn west onto Battlefield Boulevard South, Business 168 at the light opposite Gallbush Road. The Little Arrow Store is on the west corner. Pull into the parking space facing the store. There is a fee for parking and launching boats. The launching area is behind the store. For more information, call (757) 421-2561.

Put-in behind Little Arrow Store

Put-in at Bob's Fishing Hole                                                                      *vs*

## (C) *Route 168/Bob's Fishing Hole Marina*

*Directions:* From Chesapeake, Virginia drive south on Route 168/Battlefield Boulevard to about a mile south of Gallbush Road (located on the east side of 168) and turn east to get to Bob's Fishing Hole, a small marina. Be alert for the turnoff as it is south of the stoplight at Gallbush Road and Route 168 and just at the north end of the Route 168 Northwest River bridge. This stoplight also marks the current end (as of this publication date) of the Expressway/Toll Road/168 Bypass. At the turnoff, turn east, cross over the railroad tracks, and pull into the parking area near the marina's store. There is a fee for parking. Ask for the appropriate parking area and the preferred location for the launch or take-out site for canoes and kayaks.

We usually park to the south of the store and use the grassy area and very small beach there for launching or pulling out our boats. This is either the put-in or take-out, depending on the direction one wishes to paddle. To use this as the take-out, leave one car at Bob's and run a shuttle to the put-in on Bunch Walnuts Road since this river has current that flows west to east. (Bob's would be the put-in if one were doing a back and forth trip or going to Indian Creek or Smith Creek on a one-way trip.)

*Facilities:* Vending machines, a small store and a restroom are available. There is no gasoline at the marina.

Fishing at put-in at Indian Creek Road Bridge                               *vs*

## (D) *Indian Creek Road Bridge*

*Directions:* To drive to the access site at Indian Creek Road, take Gallbush Road to the east from Battlefield Boulevard. See map on page 83. Follow Gallbush east and north to Indian Creek Road and turn east. Parking for 4-6 cars is at the southeast side of the small bridge that crosses Indian Creek. On the northwest side there is room for one car.

## (E) *Smith Creek*

The Smith Creek access site is a gated site leased by the City of Chesapeake as part of Northwest River Park and is closed from sunset to 9:00 a.m.

*Directions:* To get there by automobile from Indian Creek, drive 2³⁄₁₀ miles east to Baum Road. One-tenth of a mile south on Baum Road is the entrance to Smith Creek with parking for 6 cars.

Put-in at Smith Creek                               *vs*

Put-in at Shingle Landing Creek                                    *vs*

# (F) Shingle Landing Creek

*Directions:* From NC Route 168, two miles south of the Virginia/North Carolina state line, turn northeast at the first stoplight in Moyock, North Carolina. This is Shingle Landing Road. Cross the railroad tracks and turn to the northwest (left) on SR 1222, also called Tulls Creek Road. The wooden humpback bridge, painted light gray, is there. Park where legally possible. If there are no places to park, drive back toward Route 168 and cross over it. Follow SR 1222 a short distance until it crosses the creek. There will be plenty of places to park along the small road, just avoid parking on private property. This will add just a little more time to the paddling day, but parking will be a lot easier.

*Facilities:* **Trisha's Bed & Breakfast** of Moyock, located on NC Route 168 (192 Caratoke Highway, Moyock, NC 27958), would be a delightful place to stay for a quick get-away from either the Norfolk/Virginia Beach area or the Elizabeth City area. Call for information: (252) 232-0301; www.trishasinn.com. Many of the small creeks in this part of North Carolina can be easily reached for day trips using Moyock as a home base.

---

*The greatest delight that the fields and woods minister is the suggestion of the relationship between human beings and the natural world.*

– Ralph Waldo Emerson

---

# Paddling Sections

1. **(A) Bunch Walnuts Road Bridge to (C) Route 168 /Battlefield Boulevard - Bob's Fishing Hole Marina – 6¼ miles**

2. **(B) Little Arrow Store to Northwest River – ⁶⁄₁₀ mile**

3. **(C) Route 168/Battlefield Boulevard, - Bob's Fishing Hole Marina to (D) Indian Creek Road Bridge – 3 miles**

4. **(D) Indian Creek Road Bridge to (E) Northwest River Park – 1²⁄₁₀ mile**

5. **(E) Smith Creek to Northwest River Park Dock – 1⁸⁄₁₀ mile**

6. **Northwest River Park Observation Deck to (F) Shingle Landing Creek – 4⁸⁄₁₀ mile**

7. **(F) Shingle Landing Creek to Northwest River – 1⁸⁄₁₀ mile**

8. **(F) Shingle Landing Creek to Northwest River to  Tulls Bay Marina – 9²⁄₁₀ mile**

## Section 1. (A) Bunch Walnuts Road Bridge to (C) Route 168/ Battlefield Boulevard - Bob's Fishing Hole Marina – 6¼ miles, Chesapeake, VA

This is our favorite section where the river is narrow and twists and turns a lot. It has some current and that makes it very different from most of the waterways in southeast Virginia. It is shaded for most of the way and interesting in any season.

Very shortly after leaving the wooden bridge, the Triple R Ranch comes into view. This is a summer camp with a private canoe launch and some cabins on the river. Near the Triple R Ranch, look for spoil piles that prove that the Northwest River was once dredged to this point.

Northwest River near Triple R Ranch

*vs*

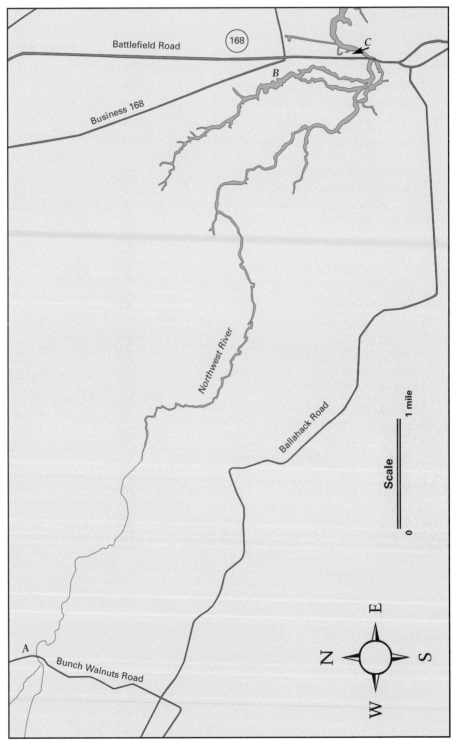

**Map 7:** Northwest River from Bunch Walnuts Road to Bob's Fishing Hole     © Vickie Shufer

Almost 1½ miles east of the bridge, there is a large clearing near a low, private bridge/road. This is an appropriate snack spot, since there is no other high ground until near the end of the trip. This is usually a portage site since the bridge is about 2½ feet above the water level. On the south side there is a former house site with only a chimney remaining. This is private property so be respectful. The river remains wooded and about 20 feet wide until within a mile or two of the take-out. Much of the land on the north shore is owned by The Nature Conservancy. It is here that Lyzer's Land is preserved. See page 92 .

Old wooden bridge crossing Northwest River                                     *vs*

## Dismal Swamp Wetlands

Near the river is the Dismal Swamp Wetlands, a 639-acre wilderness study area near the Naval Security Group Activity's facility. This research area, located in North Carolina, is managed by the Elizabeth City State University (ECSU). To access the half-mile boardwalk, call ECSU at (252) 335-3375 or the Naval Security Group, Northwest at (757) 421-8114.

## *Stewardship of the Land and Water*

A unique example of the stewardship concept is evidenced by the purchase of a tract of land adjacent to the Northwest River with funds derived from a family and group of friends to honor the life of a remarkable young woman, Elizabeth "Lyzer" McClelland. Born in Saudi Arabia of American parents, Lyzer lived most of her youth in the deserts of the Middle East. While her father was involved in diplomatic missions, Lyzer began to understand the importance of water as an extremely valuable resource. She was to graduate Cum Laude from Tufts University, designing her own degree in ecology by combining economics with geology. Earning an MA and finally a PhD in environmental sciences from the University of North Carolina, she never lost her interest in art and spent spare time drawing and painting. Last working for the EPA, she bravely fought cancer and it was her wish that her insurance money be spent preserving part of Virginia's precious wetlands.

Preserved as a legacy to her is "Lyzer's Land." Look for the bronze plaque on a tree northwest of the old wooden bridge along the river less than two miles from the Bunch Walnuts Road Bridge launch site.

The conservation strategy of protecting the land that protects the water offers a future for the terrestrial and aquatic species that depend on the balanced ecology of both. In the spring of 2003, two new land parcels along the Northwest River were transferred to The Nature Conservancy for the benefit of all of us. By using as match money the funds that Elizabeth left to The Nature Conservancy, it was possible to access a grant

source that was set aside solely to protect wetland acreage. A total of 328 acres is now protected, thanks to one woman's wish.

The authors felt especially honored to be invited to be with Lyzer's parents, Walter and Franna McClelland, and the then Director of the Green Sea Program of The Nature Conservancy, Mary Kathryn van Eerden to witness the placement of the plaque commemorating Elizabeth McClelland's dedication to preserving these wetlands for posterity.

The next landmark on the river is the tall radio tower within a mile of the take-out. The river widens as you approach the bridges on Route 168. The take-out is beyond them and the railroad bridge. Follow the bend in the river to the north and look for a small beach in the midst of some tall marsh grass on the west side of the river. The paddler's take-out car will be nearby as this is all marina property.

The Northwest River, after about 7 more miles, joins Tulls Bay and drains into Currituck Sound in North Carolina. It is from the Currituck Sound that the Northwest River sometimes receives a salty mix to its tannic waters.

Aerial view, SR 168/Northwest River      *lg*

*vs*

*lg*

## *The Northwest as a Drinking Water Source*

As of this publication date, the Northwest River is the chief water supply for part of the City of Chesapeake, Virginia. A collecting station is located adjacent to the marina, Bob's Fishing Hole, off Route 168. As much as 10 million gallons of water a day can be pumped from the river to the nearby Northwest Water Treatment Plant. This reverse-osmosis plant, dedicated on June 17, 1999, allows for the removal of salt and dissolved organic compounds. The brine and membrane concentrates from the filtration process are not pumped back into the Northwest River. They travel by residual pressure or are pumped over 15 miles to a discharge location on the Southern Branch of the Elizabeth River. Regulatory guidelines are followed to protect the receiving stream's water quality. After leaving the reverse osmosis plant, the water is further treated and disinfected following strict guidelines assuring the residents clean drinking water (Supplement to *The Virginian-Pilot*, 1999).

*Rivers connect us. They join us to our neighbors upstream and down. They link us to our past and to our future. Rivers are common bonds, even where they form boundaries. Rivers give our lives a common purpose,which, in its best manifestation, translates into environmental and historical stewardship, and into art, music and literature.*

– Canadian Heritage Rivers Board

## River Highlights

Having its origins as part of the Great Dismal Swamp, this blackwater river basin drains lands full of organic compounds. From the bridge on Bunch Walnuts Road paddling east, the river is narrow and shaded by the cypress-tupelo trees lining the banks. The best way to describe it before the leaves have fallen is "green," especially when the duckweed covers the surface of the water.

The area abounds with wildlife and several deer stands are in use on the river. Deer are quite common as are ducks, migratory songbirds, and hawks overhead. The wetland area around this part of the river is largely undeveloped and has a true wilderness feel for most of the trip. Very few houses are visible during the trip.

### Water Tupelo

A tree that is often characteristic of southern swamps, water tupelo is common along this part of the river. The base of the trunk is wide and then tapers rapidly. The purplish colored fruits, about one inch long, ripen in the fall and drop into the water, where they often collect in leaf debris and are carried downstream or deposited along the banks.

Floating Duckweed                                  *vs*

### Duckweed

Often mistaken for a blanket of green scum on ponds and waterways, duckweed is actually one of the smallest and simplest flowering plants known. A free-floating aquatic plant about ⅛ inch long, duckweeds have roots that dangle from each oval-shaped leaflike structure. Reproduction occurs mainly through cell division. It has been referred to as the math plant, since it multiplies by dividing. Each plant divides into more plants and may produce as many as twenty offspring before it dies.

97

### Hawthorn

A large shrub with red berries that ripen in the late fall, it can be distinguished from its close relative, the wild rose, by the long, stout thorns. Only a few stands exist on the river.

### Maleberry

A close relative of blueberries, it has white roundish flowers in the spring instead of bell-shaped as with blueberries. Fruits are a dry capsule containing seeds instead of a berry.

### Red Chokeberry

A small tree with fragrant white flowers in the spring followed by fruits that turn red in late fall and remain on the plant through the winter. This is a source of food for wintering birds.

vs

### Sweet Pepperbush

When most shrubs have finished blooming, this one begins, usually mid-summer with white, fragrant flowers. If you break for lunch and need to wash your hands, wet the leaves and flowers and rub them between your palms. A soapy lather will develop from the saponins contained in the plant, giving it the name "poor man's soap."

vs

### Buttonbush

A spreading shrub with many branches, it has balls of white flowers during the summer months that attract zebra swallowtails. Round, buttonlike balls of fruit follow in the fall. The seeds are consumed by ducks and other water birds. Because of its attractive foliage, it is occasionally planted as an ornamental.

# Northwest River Preserve

Located in the southern portion of Chesapeake, Virginia, more than 6,000 acres of swamps, marshes and mesic upland forests make up the Northwest River Preserve. Owned jointly by The Nature Conservancy and the Virginia Department of Conservation and Recreation, the area borders the lower reaches of the Northwest River and is a part of the "Green Sea Wetlands" located in southeastern Virginia and northeastern North Carolina.

The preserve provides year-round habitat for waterfowl, especially wood ducks and black ducks. It is especially important for migratory songbirds, providing an undeveloped expanse of land for songbirds to rest and feed before continuing on their journey. The northern parula and prothonotary warbler arrive in the spring to nest and raise their young.

A number of rare plants and animals are found here, including the silky camellia and canebrake rattlesnake in the upland forests, the Dismal Swamp southeastern shrew and epiphytic sedge in the swamps, and sawgrass, winged seedbox and little grass frog of the marshes.

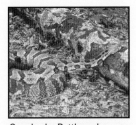
Canebrake Rattlesnake  *ps*

Silky Camellia  *vs*

Prothonotary Warbler  *vs*

*Visitation:* Presently, there are no public access facilities other than the shoreline, which can be explored by canoe or kayak. For additional information, contact Craig Young, Southeast Region Steward, Department of Conservation and Recreation, Division of Natural Heritage, Suffolk, VA (757) 925-2318 or The Nature Conservancy Green Sea Program, (757) 549-4690.

*There's no better investment in conservation than preserving and restoring wetlands. The Northwest River wetlands filter and clean Chesapeake's drinking water, provide flood control, serve as homes for birds and other wildlife, and are the nursery for young fish that mature into a recreational and commercial resource. Wetlands do all this for free. If we lose them, we're sacrificing a valuable economic resource.*

– Michael Lipford, Virginia Director for The Nature Conservancy

# History

The Northwest River, although fairly short in length, runs deep with history. It was originally one of the rivers that flowed out of the Great Dismal Swamp. Digging the Dismal Swamp Canal cut off the outflow from the Dismal Swamp (Levy, 2001). The area was explored in 1728 by William Byrd's state line survey team. Two canoes were paddled to Currituck Sound from an access point marked on Byrd's map as "North West" and "Presscot Landing." Today the spelling of the river is "Northwest," but for historical purposes and reading clarity, the authors will use the older spelling to describe the canal that was begun in 1820 and the modern spelling to refer to the river.

To provide water transport for the valuable cypress, cedar and other goods in the area to and from the Carolina Sounds and to have another route if the Dismal Swamp Canal were blocked or closed, a branch line was proposed as the North West Canal, also called the Little Canal. It had its origins in 1820 as a waste ditch for the Dismal Swamp Canal and by 1827 work was begun on a newer, wider waterway suitable for vessels up to 109 feet as long as they had a shallow draft. The canal was cut across swamplands from the Dismal Swamp beginning about a mile and a half north of the feeder ditch at Wallaceton and emptied into the Northwest River near the present-day location of the Triple R Ranch on Bunch Walnuts Road. This canal was hand dug seven miles long with three locks since the water level at the Dismal Swamp Canal was higher than the level at which the North West Canal met the Northwest River. When completed in 1831, it was twenty-four feet wide at the top and could hold water to a depth of 4 feet. It served a considerable amount of cargo as is witnessed by part of the 1833 annual report of the Dismal Swamp Canal Company which owned the North West Canal – "17,776 cubic feet of mast timber, 150,311 cubic feet of other timber, 5,773 cubic feet of plank and scantling, 737,333 hogshead staves, 455,38 long shingles, 94,775 two feet shingles, 1,224,453 building shingles, 405 cords of wood, 32,470 bushels of corn" were all transferred along the Northwest (Trout, 1998).

A description written by Alexander Crosby Brown as he was searching for remains of the old locks' outfall site in 1970 is still true.

> *One may observe that this is an exceptionally lovely, wild, but peaceful spot today, deep in the woods and completely removed from all tangible evidence of civilization including its ubiquitous harbingers of discarded paper and beer cans. The dark juniper*

*water of the canal gives the perfect reflection to the overhanging trees without revealing the slightest trace of what might lie below its tranquil surface. On a sunny April morning, with Charles Cross for guide and company, we traced the lower end of the North West Canal for a mile or so on foot down to its junction with the meandering Northwest River. This afforded time for quiet rumination on the century of 'progress' which, happily, by-passed the peaceful place entirely and also to arouse admiration for the untutored engineers whose instinctive appreciation of the laws of hydraulics contrived to make a useful waterway a thing of beauty* (Brown, 1970).

It had been the vision of early canal builders that the North West Canal would be a gateway to the Atlantic and open the area to commercial richness. This dream was short-lived as Currituck Inlet to the Atlantic Ocean closed permanently by shifting beach sands in the early 1800's. The canal did continue to be used to transport timber products to Currituck and points south, but rail travel eventually replaced the need for transport that the canals afforded.

By the end of the Civil War and a few years beyond, the North West Canal was neglected. The outfall locks and culvert were no longer in use after 1867. During the drought of 1871, to save the water in the Dismal Swamp Canal, a dam was constructed at the western terminus of the North West Canal at Wallaceton, sealing it off forever from its source. The remnants of the North West Canal and embankments today are to be seen on private property as drainage ditches. There is a portion of the original canal and outfall locks on the property of the Triple R Ranch (Trout, 1998).

The first rail line to cross the Northwest River was the Elizabeth City and Norfolk Railroad (later to be Norfolk Southern Railroad) named for the intended destinations at both ends. This line was chartered in 1870, but construction was not begun until 10 years later. On June 1, 1880 the first train traveled to Elizabeth City. By December, 1881 a total of 73 miles of tracks were laid extending the line southwest to Edenton making the Chowan River the southern terminus of the new railroad line. Freight and passengers could be transported by boat to the rail lines for the train ride to Norfolk. The economic benefits of the rail lines were extensive. Soon more tracks were laid and with improved roadways the once prolific use of waterways by steamboats, log rafts and other boats was slowly diminished (Brown, 1981).

## Section 2. (B) Little Arrow Store to Northwest River – ⁶⁄₁₀ mile, Chesapeake, Virginia

Follow the canal from the put-in to the main channel and head south to the Northwest River. Bob's Fishing Hole Marina is to the east. Even though the sound of traffic can be heard nearby, prominent marsh features can still be observed. Herons, egrets, osprey and kingfishers are good indicators of the fish population in these waters.

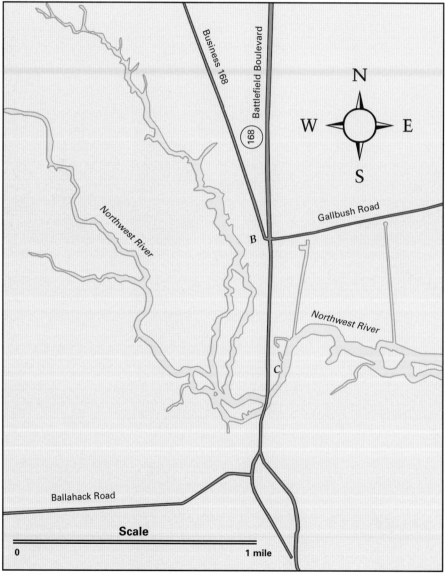

**Map 8:** Northwest River from Little Arrow Store to Bob's Fishing Hole Marina       © *Vickie Shufer*

## Nearby Historic Sites

Very near the North West Canal is the **"Ballyhack Plantation"** or **"Happer House**." Old cedar trees line one side of the lane to the house. The brick home was built in 1768 on part of the 500+ acres of land acquired through various land grants and purchases of Doctor William Happer from 1736-1751 (Hudgins, 1979, 1994, 1998). Today the house is private property. Look for this brick house on the north side of Ballahack Road near the intersection of Ballahack Road and Lake Drummond Causeway.

"Ballyhack Plantation"        Original photo by George Wallace, 1899. Collection of Larry Floyd.

At the front of the house is a large granite entry stone. Stepping into the house, one first notices the wide plank wood floors. The house also has four fireplaces, a basement, and bedrooms upstairs. Touring the outside of the home, the Flemish bond brickwork reveals part of the past. "WW Happer Dec 2 47" is carved into one of the bricks and the finger marks of the brickmaker are visible in two or more bricks as if they were freshly made (Floyd, 2003).

*Photo by George Ramsey*

Ballahack House (current spelling and current photo)          *Photo by George Ramsey*

Walking to the rear of the property, approaching the old North West Canal, an old grindstone lies in the path. The westernmost extremity of the Northwest River was known as the Ballyhack Branch. The present Ballahack Road, in Chesapeake, is named for this colonial plantation.

Within several yards of the Happer House are the remains of the North West Canal, begun in 1820. By 1827 it was lengthened to seven miles and enlarged to accommodate "lighters." These flat-bottomed boats, designed especially for shallow canals, were pulled by a mule along a towpath. Because of the differences in water depth between the Dismal Swamp Canal and the Northwest River, locks were placed measuring 24' by 111' (Ramsey, 2003). Looking at the canal today, it is amazing to imagine the amount of trade that was floated on this waterway on its way to Currituck Sound or to Norfolk.

Not far beyond the Happer House and the North West Canal is the Northwest River. It is easy to see why a canal was so useful. The Northwest River here would be impossible to navigate due to its shallow nature and the proliferation of trees. The area today is no more than a cypress swamp, hardly the waterway to be experienced at Bunch Walnuts Road Bridge and beyond.

Interestingly enough, under the dark water of a tributary of the Northwest River, lie the remains of what may be the last of the old lighters. This boat was found in 1984 and when the authors paddled there recently, it was still in place. It measures almost 90' long by the latest accounts (Ramsey, 2003). It would be a worthwhile endeavor to preserve and protect this piece of history related to the early canals.

## Section 3. (C) Route 168/Battlefield Boulevard - Bob's Fishing Hole Marina to (D) Indian Creek Road Bridge – 3 miles, one way. Chesapeake, VA

The banks of the river at this point are heavily forested with a dense understory. No development can be seen once the paddler turns her/his back on the put-in area. Even the two long straight ditches on the west side are quickly forgotten upon paddling farther. This is a perfect half-day trip or a good trip for teaching paddling skills. A canoe or kayak will feel comfortable on this short stretch. There are islands to navigate but a paddler cannot get lost on this stretch. We recommend taking the major turns to the left or north to avoid faster-moving motorboats. The only motorboats usually seen on the "paddler's side" are a few quiet fishermen. Largemouth bass, crappie, bream and catfish are the other regulars here.

Take out on the bank on the southeast side of the bridge on Indian Creek Road. This is a small informal access site, but the paddler will find it easy to land or launch from here. This land is part of the Northwest River Park and closes at sunset.

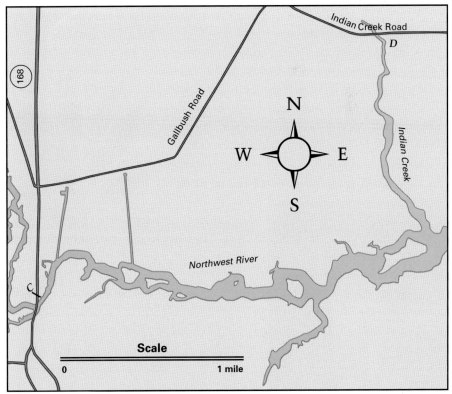

**Map 9:** Northwest River from Bob's Fishing Hole to Indian Creek Road Bridge  © Vickie Shufer

# Broad-leaved Evergreens

*We rowd' down NW River about 18 miles, as far as the Mouth of it, where it empties itself into Albemarle Sound. It was a really Delightful Sight, all the way, to see the Banks of the river adornd with Myrtle, Laurel and Bay-Trees, which preserve their Verdue the Year round, tho it must be ownd that these beautiful Plants, sacred to Venus and Appollo, grow commonly in very dirty Soil.*

*– William Byrd, 1728.*

Today the same evergreen plants continue to line the Northwest River just as they did in 1728 when Colonel William Byrd made his journey with some twenty men to survey the boundary line between Virginia and North Carolina. Waxmyrtle is the most abundant and is a medium sized shrub or small tree with leaves that are aromatic when crushed. The leaves can be used as a substitute for bay leaves in soups and stews. The berries are small, bluish-gray and grow in clusters on the branches. A waxy substance is released when boiled and was used historically to make bayberry candles and soap.

Redbay is in the Laurel family and most likely the one referred to by William Byrd as Laurel. The leaves of redbay are much larger and more leathery than those of waxmyrtle but have a similar scent when crushed. They too can be used as a substitute for bay leaves in cooking.

Sweetbay magnolia is better known for its

attractive, fragrant flowers that are white and shaped like a cup. It tends to be more of an evergreen farther south and may drop its leaves in North Carolina and Virginia if the winter is very cold. The undersides of the leaves are whitish and hairy, which help to distinguish it from the redbay.

# Section 4. (D) Indian Creek Road Bridge to Northwest River Park – 1²⁄₁₀ miles, one way. Chesapeake, VA

The access site for Indian Creek is on the southeast side of the bridge on Indian Creek Road. Fishermen frequent this area and are always willing to accommodate a paddler's need for a quick get-away. The launch area is unpaved but has a low bank making access easy for a canoe or kayak.

If water level is high enough, portage across the road and put in on the northwest side of the bridge. The river immediately forks after the put-in. Take the western fork to the left and follow the winding creek north and west as it traverses the wooded swamp. With high water it is easy to paddle over fallen trees.

Notice on some of these trees small islands have

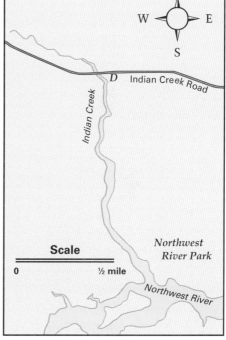

**Map 10:** Indian Creek                    © Vickie Shufer

developed. Interesting plants grow in these micro habitats. An odd looking plant on the upper section of Indian Creek is the sprawling, twining, parasitic plant known as dodder. The orange, string-like stems have no leaves or roots and lack chlorophyll, which helps plants manufacture food from sunlight. Instead, the plant attaches

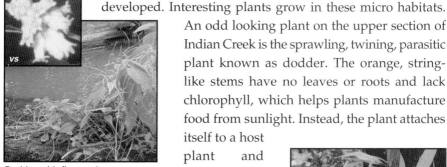

Dodder with flower close-up        lg

itself to a host plant and absorbs the energy, nutrients and water from that plant.

During the summer, look for the beautiful orange flowers of the Turk's cap lily, one of the few places where we have seen it growing. Soon you will find that fallen trees and debris block the way and it will be time to turn back.

Turk's Cap Lily        lg

## Early Settlers on Indian Creek

Often, it is interesting to trace the origin of a creek's name or find a tidbit of historical interest about it. While researching the history of Indian Creek in the land patent books for Virginia, one finds dozens of creeks by that name. To find a reference to this particular Indian Creek seemed to lead to nothing but dead-ends. However, by looking for a reference to Currituck, the colonial ownership of this small creek was revealed. In a patent dated October 20, 1691, Joel Martin received 1500 acres "on a Cyprus Sw. of the uper Indian Cr. of the north west river; in Corrotuck Precincts; at time of survey in Low. Norf. Co; adj. Malder's land" (Nugent, 1977). That this land adjoined another named settler's land indicates that colonial habitation along Indian Creek may have occurred at least by 1691.

Once at the bridge, portage across and continue south toward Northwest River. The paddling here is hardly ever crowded. There are a few motorboats, mostly slow moving, but in warm weather several personal watercraft can be seen (or heard). From the Northwest River, along the southern boundary of the park, the only signs of development are two waterfront structures. The Marjorie Rein Memorial Walkway, which ends at an elevated wooden deck overlooking the Northwest River, is accessed from the southern end of the park. The park's low dock located to the east of the Marjorie Rein Memorial Walkway is at the water's edge and provides easy access for canoes and kayaks. There are vending machines, restrooms, and a mowed grassy area nearby making this a great picnic spot. The park does not allow the use of this dock as a public put-in site for a river trip. Launching is for canoes being portaged from the park's man-made lake to the Northwest River.

Bee Dee McMillan and friend at the dock at the southern end of Northwest River Park          *vs*

# River Highlights

The creek bank is shaded by water tupelo and bald cypress trees. You will see a colony of water lilies soon after leaving sight of the bridge. The lily pads become a microhabitat for frogs, young turtles and insects. In the spring, look for the bright yellow sundrops, blue flags, and the heart-shaped leaves of the arrow arum. As you approach Northwest River Park, black willow trees, waxmyrtles, and other shrubs form a dense understory bordering the river. Sweetflag and cattails grow at the water's edge while groundnuts and leather flower, with its beautiful purple flowers, climb into the shrubs.

Fragrant Water Lily          vs

Leather Flower          vs

Black Willow flowers          vs

Black Willow cotton          vs

## Cotton

About the middle of May, the Northwest River dons a layer of white cotton floating on its surface. Closer observation reveals the source as the black willow trees lining the shoreline. After pollination seed capsules develop, each one containing several seeds embedded in the cotton fluff. As the seed capsule matures, it splits open, releasing the cotton and dispersing its seeds to be carried by the wind to new sites.

Lloyd Goodbread and friend on a sunny day at Northwest River Park          vs

Aerial view of Northwest River Park          *City of Chesapeake, Parks & Recreation Department*

## *Northwest River Park*

Paddling south from the put-in, the 763-acre Northwest River Park comes into view immediately on the east bank. This beautiful woodland park is operated by the city of Chesapeake and contains a 70-site campground open April 1 to December 1. The day use areas, open year-round from 9 a.m. until sunset, feature picnic areas and shelters, an equestrian area for horse owners, miniature golf, the Memorial Garden, a fragrance garden for the visually impaired, hiking trails, a ropes course area and a small lake and canal for canoe and paddleboat rentals. A camp store, vending machines and restrooms are available. Access to the Northwest River is from the launch site at the bridge on Indian Creek Road, or from Smith Creek, located off Baum Road, maintained by the Northwest River Park. See park map on page 109. For more information, contact Northwest River Park, 1733 Indian Creek Road, Chesapeake, VA 23322, (757) 421-3145 or 421-7151 or visit the web site at www.chesapeake.va.us.

| Walking Trails | Miles |
|---|---|
| (1) Indian Creek | 2.5 |
| (2) Molly Mitchell | 1.5 |
| (3) Wood Duck Slough | 0.5 |
| (4) Otter Point | 1.0 |
| (5) Marjorie Rein | .25 |
| (6) Shuttle Trail | 1.25 |
| (7) Deer Island | .75 |

Northwest River Park Trail Map

*Drawing by Lauren Gansemer*

## Section 5. (E) Smith Creek to Northwest River Park - 1⁸⁄₁₀ miles, one way. Chesapeake, VA

This is an excellent access site for small boats. The only drawback is low water following a sustained northwest wind. This access is not paved, but the bank is gently sloped making it very easy to launch a canoe or kayak and push off from the shore.

This is a very small tributary of the Northwest, but an attractive paddling spot with a lot of birding to be done here. Pull into one of the smaller inlets and look for turtles sunning on logs and listen for the myriad bird songs. The creek has a few turns and has been called "Crooked Creek" on some older maps. At the juncture of Smith Creek and the Northwest River, it is possible to paddle into North Carolina by heading south or follow the shoreline on the

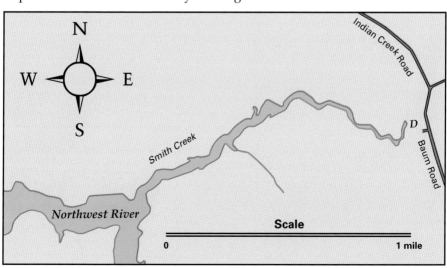

**Map 11:** Smith Creek to Northwest River

© *Vickie Shufer*

north to get to the observation deck/dock at Northwest River Park.

On the return trip, heading east on Smith Creek, be sure to take the right fork just after the junction with the Northwest River. As landmarks along the route, look for a rather large cypress tree with low branches and many cypress knees on the north and some cleared land beyond the trees on the south side of the river. There is a dock on private property near the clearing. After several turns, when the creek appears to divide, follow the larger stream to the north. The stream again divides to the north and east. Take the eastern turn and the take-out point is not far. At this point the creek is quite narrow until the take-out site is seen. If a wrong turn is taken, simply retrace the path and turn at the correct spot. The short spurs either dead-end or are too debris-filled to paddle. This is a gated access point controlled by Northwest River Park and is closed from sunset to 9:00 a.m.

## River Highlights

Before launching your canoe or kayak, take a few moments to listen and observe the natural sights and sounds. Woodpeckers chip away on the trunks of old and dying trees in their quest for food. Kingfishers make a ratchety call as they depart from their perch on branches overhanging the creek. Turtles bask in the sunlight on fallen logs before splashing into the water at the first hint of being approached. Great blue herons keep a safe distance with short, frequent flights ahead of the paddler.

Swamp blackgum fruits vs

Bordering the creek are bald cypress, water tupelo and swamp blackgum trees that provide shade for most of the way to the Northwest River. The large buttresses stablilize the trees in water. Swamp rose, swamp dogwood, and red chokeberry provide support for the greenbriers and other vines. Royal ferns emerge from the mucky soil and in the spring sundrops add a bright yellow hue to the dark waters. During the fall and winter, after the leaves have dropped, look up into the branches for patches of green. Mistletoe and resurrection fern are among the plants that grow on plants.

### Mistletoe

Mistletoe is a parasitic plant that gets its nutrients from the host tree on which it grows. Even though the berries are poisonous to humans, birds eat them and pass the undigested seed through their system. The seed is sticky and adheres to the branches of trees, takes root, and grows.

vs

112

## Plant and Animal Relationships

Waxmyrtle shrubs produce berries that are a food source for the yellow-rumped warbler, who arrives in the fall when the berries ripen, and leaves in the spring. The berries from the swamp blackgum are one of the favorite foods of black bears and evidence of their presence can be seen on the bald cypress trees.

Yellow-rumped warbler          *vs*

### Bear Signs

Black bears use swamps and waterways as corridors, linking them to natural areas where they feed and reproduce. You may not see the bear, but you can see where the bear has been. Claw marks are left on trees and bark is stripped from the trunk. American Indians of the southeast would locate bears by looking for their claw marks and would find females hibernating in the tops of hollow trees (Hudson, 1976).

*vs*

*vs*

### Old Man's Beard

The long, gray-green wispy strands that look like green spanish moss hanging from the branches are actually lichens. Not really a "plant," a lichen is a combination of an alga and a fungus living together in a symbiotic relationship. The fungus provides a rigid structure on which chlorophyll-bearing algae spread out and provide food for both. Lichens are air indicators, growing best in non-polluted areas.

113

## Section 6. Northwest River Park's Observation Deck to (F) Shingle Landing Creek, Moyock, NC - 4⁸⁄₁₀ miles, one way. Chesapeake, VA and Currituck County, NC

Paddlers, please note that the park's observation deck/dock is not a public launch site for anyone except for park canoe renters portaging from the park's man-made lake to the Northwest River. We are simply using it as a reference point for mileage.

Use the access point for either Smith Creek or Indian Creek. If paddling from Smith Creek, head south following the larger section of the Northwest River. If paddling from Indian Creek, follow the creek south to the Northwest River, pass the observation deck/dock at Northwest River Park, then head south.

After paddling across the VA/NC state line, the land to the east of the river is the Northwest River Marsh Black Bear Sanctuary. This bear sanctuary extends to some of the marsh on the west side as well. There is some private property interspersed among acreage belonging to the state. The entrance to Shingle Landing Creek is almost a mile from the Virginia/North Carolina State line. It may be difficult to determine by water, but it is the fifth creek on the west side of the river, heading south from the junction of Smith Creek and the Northwest River. The paddler will also notice that the Northwest River makes a hard turn to the east at the juncture with Shingle Landing Creek. Follow Shingle Landing Creek for two miles to the take-out at the humpback bridge in Moyock, North Carolina, at SR 1222/Tulls Creek Road. For a complete description of Shingle Landing Creek, see page 114.

This section of the river has a lot to offer the explorer by boat. There are many unnamed small creeks and inlets along this route and the shoreline changes from forest to mostly marsh.

## *River Highlights*

The marsh that borders the Northwest River is a tidal freshwater marsh. Tides are greatly influenced by the wind direction. Rapidly spreading through the marsh is Phragmites, a non-native grass that threatens native species. Also growing along the shoreline are big cordgrass, black needlerush and cattails. Bulltongue, pickerelweed, arrow arum, royal fern and marsh fern are interspersed among them.

Big Cordgrass inflorescence                    *vs*

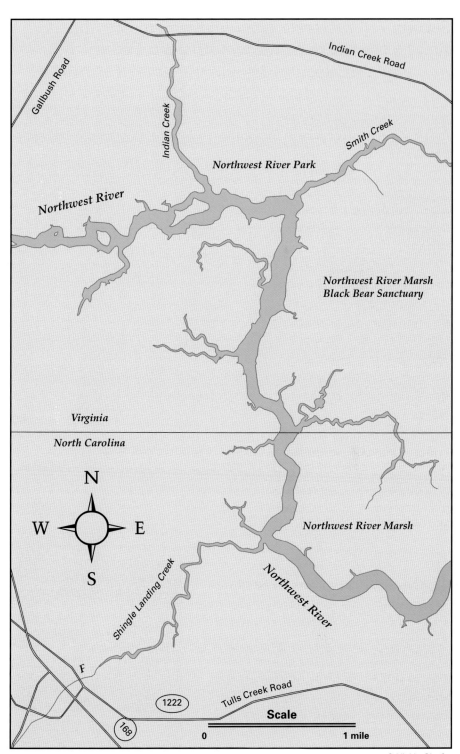

**Map 12:** Northwest River Park to Shingle Landing Creek

© Vickie Shufer

115

## Section 7. (F) Shingle Landing Creek to Northwest River - 1⁸⁄₁₀ miles, one way. Currituck County, NC

This is an informal access point, unpaved, but easy for a canoe or kayak. Paddle east from the humpback bridge along this narrow, shady creek. This is a beautiful route in a hardwood swamp that widens slowly until it meets the Northwest River.

We have found no public landing sites along this route so be prepared to eat a snack or lunch while afloat in canoe or kayak. The presence of a few houses and a private farm road do not mar the paddling enjoyment of this quiet creek.

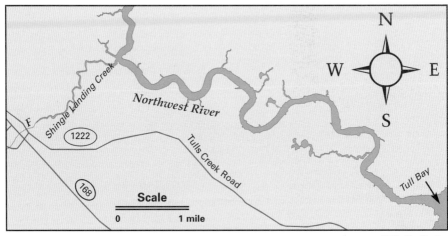

**Map 13:** Shingle Landing Creek to Northwest River to Tull Bay                    © *Vickie Shufer*

Humpback Bridge, Shingle Landing Creek

116

*vs*

## River Highlights

Greeting us at the put-in at Shingle Landing Creek were the barn swallows, the acrobats of the air. Rather than using a barn to build their mud and daub nests, they had used the underside of the bridge. The flight movements are for more than entertainment as they are actually catching and feeding on mosquitoes, gnats and other flying insects.

Blue Flag                              vs

Sweet Flag                             vs

This is a freshwater swamp with bald cypress trees lining the shores. Highbush blueberries, swamp sweetbells and other members of the heath family grow in the understory. Isolated stands of blue flag and sweetflag can be found. The blue flag is actually an iris and has large purplish flowers in the spring. The leaves are a darker green than the sweetflag which tends to have a yellow green color. The sweetflag is a member of the arum family, not related to the iris at all. Its flower is a small greenish spadix about midway up the stalk and is easily missed. The leaves emit a fragrant scent when crushed and were once used by early settlers as an air freshener.

## *1920's Mint*

The rich farmland of Currituck County near Moyock was part of a Mennonite experiment in agriculture that might have proven extremely profitable if it had continued. Joseph Slabaugh in 1920 planted an acre in peppermint and erected a small distillery. The result of his efforts produced pure oil of peppermint. It is said that this first batch was stored in the vault of the Bank of Currituck until a steel storage drum arrived for shipping. The oil was insured for $5,000 with a gallon valued at $800.00. A dissention within the Mennonite Church is credited with the dissolution of the mint business as these Mennonites sold their land and moved away (Welch, 1982).

# Moyock History

In the Library of Congress are two maps that indicate Shingle Landing Creek was named Moyock Creek in the years 1760 and 1765. An American Indian word, Moyock is said to mean "Place of oak on the trail" (Currituck County Bicentennial Committee, 1976). The town of Moyock was also called Shingle Landing and Moyock Creek became Shingle Landing Creek. Both were named for the product cut and processed nearby from the then ample supply of cedar and cypress trees in Currituck County.

In the early 1700's a coastal storm opened an inlet at the northern end of Currituck Sound connecting to the Atlantic Ocean. Before the advent of reliable roads and the invention of the steam engine locomotive, travel by water provided the easiest transportation mode for heavy lumber and wood products. The serendipitous storm opening facilitated the development of Shingle Landing into a thriving seaport, for a while. Shingles, barrel staves and other wood products were shipped directly from Shingle Landing Creek in vessels bound for ports including the West Indies (Trout, 1998). The inlet closed permanently before the mid 1800's, but timbering continued in the area with the shipping channels being the Dismal Swamp Canal via the Northwest River and later the Albemarle and Chesapeake Canal.

When the first post office opened in 1857, the official name of the community became Moyock. By 1880 the railroad reached the village of

Vandecah's Store and Cotton Gin, Moyock, NC                    *Collection of Melinda Lukei*

Moyock and boosted construction of homes and businesses along its route. By 1910 Shingle Landing Creek was dredged to accommodate the larger boats arriving from the Outer Banks with cargoes of fish and oysters (Welch, 1982). These cargoes could then be shipped by rail to Norfolk. Several old homes from the late 1800's and early 1900's and the former **Poyner Store** are adjacent to the old port of Shingle Landing in a three block historical area along the railroad line that is now Norfolk and Southern.

It's interesting to consider the history of Shingle Landing Creek looking at its current size. At fairly low water, remnants of a corduroy road and old landing can still be seen not far from the confluence with the Northwest River. The paddler may find that paddling in almost complete silence, except for the occasional bird or frog, some of the trees sound against each other in the wind. It's an eerie noise, which conjures up thoughts of ghost rafts of creaking logs being hauled along the small waterway.

The former Poyner Store is now head-quarters for Currituck Realty Company    *vs*

# Section 8. (E) Shingle Landing Creek to Northwest River to Tulls Bay Marina – 9²⁄₁₀ miles one way. Currituck County, NC

Access this final part of the Northwest River by putting in at Moyock, North Carolina at the humpback bridge on SR 1222/Tulls Creek Road to the Northwest River. Since there is no take-out on Tulls Bay the authors advise either going into Tulls Bay and take out at Tulls Bay Marina or return to the Moyock access site. Although going into Tulls Bay Marina will add 2 more miles to the paddling trip, the paddler will find the take-out at the marina a welcome sight to end a long paddling day. Plan ahead and leave a car at the marina. Check with the attendant or utilize the honor system collecting box for fees.

After the junction with Shingle Landing Creek, the Northwest River takes a turn to the southeast. From here to the opening at Tulls Bay, the river is about 1/10 of a mile wide. There are a few stands of pine trees and wide marshes bordering the river. This can be a long trip by canoe and the authors prefer to paddle here in kayaks. The water on Tulls Bay is usually flat even when wind kicks up on the North Landing River and Currituck Sound, both of which are nearby. This makes for comfortable paddling, but also attracts water skiers and personal watercraft in warm weather.

There are a few good lunch spots, so take advantage of them as you find them. Nellie Bell Ponds is one of the inlets that can be explored if the water level is not too low. Be aware of private property. There are no public access points here. The Northwest River Marsh Black Bear Sanctuary is on the north side of the river, extending north to the Virginia line. Parts of the sanctuary are also on the south or west side as the river turns and finally meets Tulls Bay. The western end of Tulls Bay is also part of the sanctuary. See map on page 113.

After entering Tulls Bay, follow the western shoreline. To get to Tulls Bay Marina by boat, look for the opening to the last creek before going under the bridge at Tulls Creek Bridge. In other words, if you get to a bridge, turn around and look for a small creek to the west. This is a short paddle trip on a canal to the take-out.

For more paddling information on Tulls Bay and its tributaries, please see the next chapter.

## Sligo

Sligo, North Carolina is located about 8 miles south of Moyock and has a name whose origins many have pondered. Reading an information booklet from the bicentennial celebration of Currituck County, the mystery is solved. An interesting tale about the name is that of a visitor of many years ago who stood at the intersection that marks the community's center. He is believed to have said, "S'll I go this way or S'll I go that way?" Charming, but not accurate according to the researchers who put together the booklet. They claim the true naming came from a Methodist minister who was a Circuit rider from Sligo Island, Ireland. The gentleman was Edward Drumgoole, who frequented the area in 1783 (Currituck Bicentennial Committee, 1976). Even if his last name had been chosen, the village would still have an interesting name.

Part Five

# Currituck Waterways

# Tulls Bay and Tributaries

The Northwest River is the largest tributary of Tulls Bay as it slowly flows into the lake-like bay. Tulls Bay is shallow, only about 4 feet deep for most of its two mile breadth. At its widest point it is about three miles. Tulls Bay has many developments along its shoreline. The marshland seen to the north from Tulls Bay is actually an island and the last fragment of the Northwest River as it gently curves around the north side.

Three small creeks to the south and west of Tulls Bay combine to form Tulls Creek. These small creeks include Roland Creek and Roland Creek Canal to the west and Buckskin Creek and Cowells Creek to the south near Sligo, NC. From the "mouth" of

## Location

Just about 2 miles south of the NC/VA state line, Tulls Bay is located in Currituck County and is the link between the North Landing River to the east and the Northwest River to the northwest. Northwest River Marsh Game Land is on the northern and western border.

## Access Points

A. **Tulls Bay Marina**

B. **Tulls Creek**

C. **Currituck, NC**

Tulls Bay, the paddler can venture into the path of the Intracoastal Waterway and the end of the North Landing River as it widens into Currituck Sound.

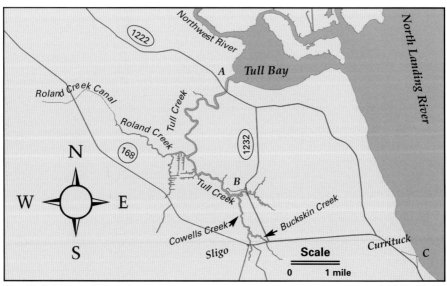

**Map 14:** Tull Bay and tributaries

© Vickie Shufer

## Access Points
## (A) Tulls Bay Marina

*Directions:* Tulls Bay Marina is on SR 1222/Tulls Creek Road, about 5 miles from Moyock or 3½ miles from Sligo, NC. From Route 168, at the northern end of Moyock, turn northeast at the first stoplight. Cross the railroad tracks and turn southeast on Tulls Creek Road. Go about 5 miles. Tulls Bay Marina will be on the north side of the road. There is a boat launching fee with a box out front to collect money if no one is there. Do abide by the honor system.

Tulls Bay Marina                                                                                    vs

### Tull or Tulls?

While neither author has ever heard anyone who refers to the creek or bay by the name, "Tull," we are using that name instead of "Tulls" on the map because it is the official name used on road maps, charts, and topographic quadrant maps. When speaking of the area in the text, we still call the creek and the bay, "Tulls," which rings truer to the ear and is the locals' term. An old habit is hard to break.

## (B) Tulls Creek

The access for motorized and non-motorized boats is at Poyners Road Community Park near the village of Sligo, North Carolina. There are multiple put-in spots for canoes or kayaks along the banks.

*Directions:* Drive east from Sligo on Route 168 less than ½ mile, then turn north on SR 1232/Poyners Road. Go a little over a mile until you cross a small bridge and see a community park on the west side of the road. Park where convenient. There is ample parking for several cars, including space for boat trailers.

*Facilities:* There are no restroom facilities at this park, but picnic tables are available. Docks and a boat ramp are adjacent to the parking area.

Susan Snyder launching kayak at Poyners Road Community Park                    *vs*

## (C) Currituck, NC

The last access site for paddling into Tulls Bay is in the village of Currituck, North Carolina near the North Carolina Department of Transportation (NCDOT) Ferry Landing. We were advised by a NCDOT employee that the only approved launch site is the very small sandy beach topped by granite rip-rap. This location is just to the north of the picnic tables near the ferry landing. We were advised by the same NCDOT employee that using the sandy beach behind the two story private home is considered trespassing and anyone using that site is subject to arrest.

*Directions:* From Sligo drive east on Route 168 3²/₁₀ miles. Look for Courthouse Road angling to the southeast at the gas station. Follow this road a short distance to the village of Currituck. Be careful not to park in the lanes marked for the ferry or on private property. There may be a little parking along the roadway. After finding a spot to park, walk to the north side of the ferry landing property and look for a small sandy beach topped with granite rip-rap. At high water levels, no sand will be visible and this could be treacherous. This is the only public take-out spot available until the North Carolina Wildlife Resources Commission Boat Ramp is reached at Waterlily, near Coinjock, approximately 6 miles by water. There is a private boat ramp on Bell Island about 4 miles from Currituck. See page 136 for more information. Do not trespass on private property and do not use the ferry landing. Be forewarned, the NCDOT employees take their jobs very seriously and it may be prudent to ask for permission to launch or land a canoe or kayak. Call (252) 232-2075 for more information.

*Facilities*: Currituck/Knotts Island Ferry, NCDOT property has two picnic tables available for public use with very limited parking. Do not park in the ferry lane parking areas and do not attempt to put in or take out in the ferryboat's launching/landing area. The free ferry leaves Currituck for Knotts Island 6 times a day. For information go to www.ncferry.org or call (252) 232-2075.

Canoe/Kayak launch site at high water

*vs*

# Paddling Sections

1. **(A) Tulls Bay Marina to North Landing River/Intracoastal Waterway - 4½ miles**

2. **(B) Tulls Creek to Tulls Bay - 4⅓ miles**

3. **(B) Tulls Creek to Roland Creek**

4. **Mouth of Tulls Bay (North Landing River) to (C) Currituck, NC - 2⁴⁄₁₀ miles**

## *Section 1. (A) Tulls Bay Marina to North Landing River/Intracoastal Waterway - 4½ miles, one way. Currituck County, NC*

This paddle trip is interesting in that the paddler travels from a narrow entrance creek into a large body of water (Tulls Bay) that resembles a lake. The water is dark and brackish, not very salty. This is a great place to swim, as the bottom is sandy and shallow. Paddling east across Tulls Bay to the North Landing River /Intracoastal Waterway might be an arduous trip for a canoe on a windy day and there is no public take-out point on Tulls Bay. The trip can be an out-and-back trip or cn end at the small beach on NCDOT property just to the north of the Currituck/Knotts Island Ferry Landing described on page 122.

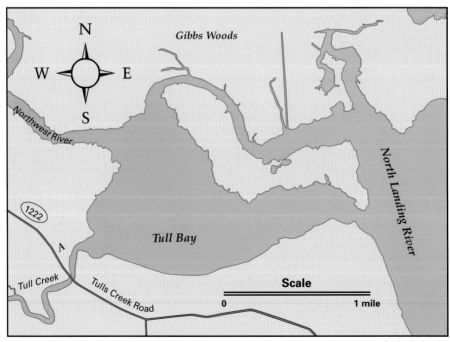

**Map 15:** Tull Bay to North Landing River                    © Vickie Shufer

Tulls Bay is bordered on the south by houses and what remains of the few farms that attest to its agricultural heritage. On the northwest end is (appropriately) the Northwest River. On the eastern end, Tulls Bay opens into the North Landing River/Intracoastal Waterway. The North Landing River then joins Currituck Sound, which leads south to the mouth of Albemarle Sound.

The marshland visible to the north of Tulls Bay is an island with little solid ground referred to as Sampson's Island in a 1687 land grant to John Gibbs (Nugent, 1977). The entrance to the Northwest River is at the west end of the island. The land to the north of the river on the north side of the island is Gibbs Woods. To the east of Tulls Bay across the North Landing River are Mackay Island and Knotts Island. These areas east of Tulls Bay have some remarkable history and will be discussed in the third book in the series of Wild River Guides.

## *Gibbs Woods*

The plantation of Gibbs Woods was named for Captain John Gibbs who was governor of the County of Albemarle for at least one session of the General Assembly (Pugh, 1973). A land patent for 3100 acres was recorded for Captain Gibbs in October of 1687 and he had a house and an established plantation there by that date (Nugent, 1977). Today Gibbs Woods is considered the land bordered by the Northwest River to the south and west, the North Landing to the east, and the Virginia state line to the north.

According to local tradition, when the boundary line for North Carolina and Virginia was surveyed in 1728, it cut right through Mr. Gibbs' house, making his porch in Virginia and the rest of the house in North Carolina. His wife remarried in 1702 and it is assumed that this was the year of his death. In 1774, an advertisement in the Virginia Gazette listed the property for sale by Gibbs' grandson (Pugh, 1973).

### *River Highlights*

The narrow blackwater creek/canal leading from the marina is usually a good location to spot great blue herons and a few wading birds. It's a short trip (½ mile) to the southwest end of Tulls Bay.

The marshes to the north of Tulls Bay are part of a complex system of tidal freshwater marshes dominated by phragmites, big cordgrass, cattails, and black needlerush. Ospreys are frequently seen flying overhead during the summer months. Snakes are also common in the spring and summer.

Keep an eye open for the cottonmouth, a poisonous water snake, floating on top of the water. Non-poisonous water snakes swim with their bodies submerged.

During the fall and winter, the quiet of the marshes is broken by a loud honking sound as swans and geese fly overhead, usually in V-formation. Tundra swans are the largest of the waterfowl and are completely white birds with a black bill. The long neck is extended and the wings are located near the rear of the body. Snow geese are also large white birds, but in flight show black wing tips that distinguish them from the swans. Canada geese have a black head, white chin patch and a pale breast.

The waterfowl population arrives in October and November to spend winters in northeastern North Carolina and southeastern Virginia. Their stay is fairly short. By the end of January, on the first warm day, they begin the return journey to the north.

Snow Goose

Canada Goose

Tundra Swan

## Land of the Wild Goose

The word "Currituck" was originally an Algonquian Indian word, "Coratank," thought to mean "wild goose." During the winter migratory season, thousands of Canada Geese, swans, and many varieties of ducks still frequent the area. The name "Currituck" has endured no less than twenty different spellings over many years on maps and legal documents. An opening to the Atlantic Ocean has been given a variation of the Currituck name that has existed since the 1600's. A map dated about 1685 identifies "Caratuck Inlet" at 36 degrees and 30 minutes. The earliest written references to Currituck are in a letter dated May 8, 1654 that spells the name as "Carotoke," a charter dated June 30, 1665 which uses the spelling "Currituck" (Wood, 1974), and a land patent from September 10, 1664 uses the name "Curratuck" (Nugent, 1992). The current spelling seems to have been adopted in 1765 (Currituck Council Tricentennial Committee, 1970).

# North Carolina or Virginia?

William Byrd (1674-1744), in his *History of the Dividing Line*, explained that most of the "Northern American Continent now under the Dominion of the King of Great Britain, and Stretching quite as far as the Cape of Florida, went at first under the General Name of Virginia" (Byrd, 1728). By royal decrees from the King, New England was pared off Virginia in 1628; the colony of Maryland, in 1632; North Carolina (then called "Carolina"), in 1663.

In squabbles largely over taxes, land rights, and commerce, citizens complained to the governors of Carolina and Virginia and word was sent to the Lords Proprietors of North Carolina and the King that a true boundary line needed to be determined. Upon official decree, Governor Everard of North Carolina and Governor Spotswood of Virginia appointed a group of commissioners and surveyors to determine the line, map it, and measure distances. In March, 1728, the Virginia group of three commissioners, at least two servants for the commissioners, two surveyors, a chaplain and about fifteen outdoorsmen, each armed with a musket and tomahawk or large hatchet, was outfitted with tents and various supplies. They met up with the Carolina group at the old Currituck Inlet on the Atlantic coast. This group discussed and agreed on a starting point, took bearings, placed a cedar stake in the ground, and began their unusual journey. Along the way, they would hunt for meat and buy food from the settlers or the American Indians they would encounter. This was the first recorded trip of non-native men to walk through the Dismal Swamp.

William Byrd, one of the Commissioners from Virginia chosen to determine the boundary line between Virginia and North Carolina, describes the journey from beginning to end in a remarkable set of documents, *History of the Dividing Line and The Secret History*. The sixteen week, several hundred mile journey from Currituck Inlet marching westward was an arduous one: roadless, uncharted and some areas uninhabited. The group of about twenty men walked, rode horses, paddled canoes, camped under the stars or stayed at locals' houses and barns. The *History of the Dividing Line* was the "official" book that was to be published, but *The Secret History* was Byrd's very private and revealing diary. Anyone with a remote interest in history will enjoy this look at a most unusual expedition. They have been reprinted by Dover Publications in a single volume. Look for the title, *Histories of the Dividing Line betwixt Virginia and North Carolina*, by William Byrd.

## Section 2. (B) Tulls Creek to Tulls Bay – 4⅓ miles, one way. Currituck County, NC

The man-made canal beginning at Poyners Road Community Park is a small tree-lined waterway that leads west and north to the larger Tulls Creek. It is possible to paddle a short distance on Cowells Creek and Buckskin Creek if one turns to the south upon leaving the feeder creek. See map on page 129 to see how these creeks intersect. To reach Tulls Bay, follow Tulls Creek for almost 1½ miles to the northwest until you come to a fork in the creek. Turning to the north, Tulls Creek winds its way to Tulls Bay. To the west, Roland Creek (also called Rowland Creek) can be followed for several miles. This water trail ends at Tulls Bay right after the paddler passes under the bridge of SR 1222/Tulls Creek Road. See map, page 129. The few houses seen along the way do not detract from this largely wilderness water trail. This is a fine creek that is not the least bit boring to use as an out-and-back trip.

## River Highlights

Tulls Creek is a small blackwater creek and a great fishing spot. The locals report catching striped bass, perch and crappie. Much of Tulls Creek is bordered by marshes. Several signs posted by the North Carolina Department of Transportation indicate that this is a "Wetland Research Site." A few stands of non-native phragmites can be seen on the south side while on the north side are native sawgrass communities. Rose mallows and bull-tongue are interspersed among the grasses and sedges. A young forest dominated by pines borders the creek near the put-in but then is replaced by young bald cypress trees farther west.

Molly, Ryan and Jacob Lavender fishing at Poyners Road Community Park                    *vs*

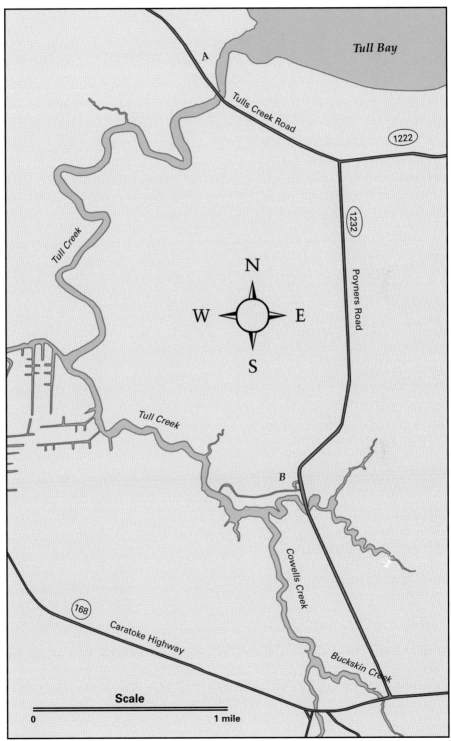

**Map 16:** Tull Creek

© Vickie Shufer

## Section 3. (B) Tulls Creek to Roland Creek – mileage variable. Currituck County, NC

As a tributary of Tulls Creek, Roland Creek heads northwest at the spot where Tulls Creek turns north to join Tulls Bay. Follow the route that appears to be more or less a straight route. If taking a sharp turn to the southwest, the paddler is now entering either Guinea Mill Run Canal (the first hard turn to the southwest) or Roland Creek Canal (the more westerly of the "hard turns.") It is obvious that the creek and the canals have been dredged as there are spoil banks on one side of the creek. We are told that these were early canals used for the transport of timber products. Paddle as far as time will allow or until deadfall prevents going any further.

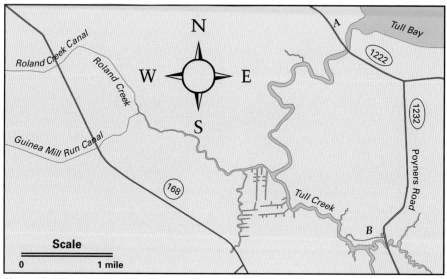

**Map 17:** Tull Creek to Roland Creek    © Vickie Shufer

## River Highlights

Soon after entering Roland Creek, look for the cypress tree that looks "different." From a distance, the color is a lighter green, the needles are shorter and pressed against the stem and it has a more wispy look than its cousin, also standing nearby. This is the pond cypress, a southern species found in swamps in Georgia and Florida, which reaches

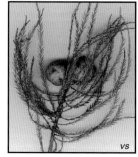

its northern limits in northeastern North Carolina. Like the bald cypress, the pond cypress is also deciduous, revealing its reddish-brown bark in the winter months.

## Section 4. Mouth of Tulls Bay (NLR) to (C) Currituck, NC - 2 ⁴/₁₀ miles. Currituck County, NC

From the "mouth" of Tulls Bay, at its eastern end, the paddler can venture into the path of the Intracoastal Waterway and the end of the North Landing River as it widens into Currituck Sound. Sailboats, yachts large and small, barges and small freight carriers all use this Intracoastal Waterway. The long fetch of the waterway combined with the depth of the Intracoastal channel can create some powerful waves. Paddlers beware! Do check the weather before planning to continue on the waterway into this wide section of the North Landing River as it merges with Currituck Sound.

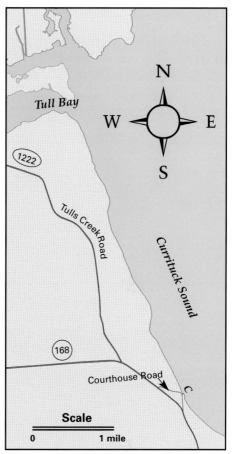

**Map 18:** Tull Bay to Currituck     © Vickie Shufer

Osprey, Laughing Gulls and Ring-billed Gull      vs

133

## River Highlights

The focus on this part of the river is mainly on paddling and being observant of other watercraft on the river. Overhead, seagulls, terns, vultures, osprey and herons are some of the more common birds to watch for in the warmer months. In the fall cormorants, geese, swans and ducks can be spotted. Closer to shore are rushes, big cordgrass, rose mallows, groundsel bush and other flowering plants.

## *History*

The creek and bay were named for an early settler, Thomas Tull whose house served as a courthouse when needed. "A precinct court was held at ye house of Thos. Tulle, Esq., in Currituck Apl. 22nd, 1695" (Hathaway, 1900). Tull's son, Benjamin Tull, probably lived in Currituck in 1699, as papers found in the Camden Courthouse record "John Bennett sold a servant girl in 1699 to Benjamin Tulle in Currituck" (Hathaway, 1900). In 1703 Benjamin is listed as a resident as noted in a legal paper concerning a lawsuit with Colonel William Reed. An interesting historic note is that a descendant of William Reed is the U.S. Army surgeon Dr. Walter Reed (1851-1902) who investigated the causes of yellow fever. This famous gentleman of Currituck ancestry had the distinction of having the Walter Reed Army Medical Center in Washington, DC named in his honor (Wright, 1973). Back in the eighteenth century, Benjamin Tull lost the lawsuit with William Reed. Other written information concerning Mr. Benjamin Tull were in 1710 when he was named a vestryman for the parish and in 1728 a notation was made concerning his vessel which was carrying guns and ammunition (The Historical Committee, 1970).

Another note of interest is the mention of watercraft in almost all of the early wills from the residents of Currituck County. It seems that every family owned some sort of boat. There were many varieties used for fishing, hunting, commerce, and transportation. Because early roads were few and movement on them slow and arduous, water transportation made excellent sense. The people of the region were (and some still are) intimately connected to the rivers, creeks, bays, and sounds for almost every aspect of their lives. Watercraft named in the wills include schooners (a total of forty between 1760 and 1840 alone!), punts, canoes, boats, small boats, and pilot boats (Currituck County Bicentennial Committee. 1976).

# Historic Sites

**Pilmoor Memorial Methodist Church**, built in 1928, is named in honor of Joseph Pilmoor who preached the first Methodist sermon in North Carolina in 1772 (Pritchard, 1965). The church is famous for introducing what may have been the first church bus in the United States. Named the *Miss Memorial*, this 48 passenger Ford made her maiden trip on July 5, 1931 and by 1933 the experimental innovation paid off as the church membership doubled over these two years (Pritchard, 1965). The **Pilmoor Church** can be seen from Currituck Sound as the paddler approaches the ferry landing site at the village of Currituck. Other historic structures are the **Currituck County Courthouse**, originally established in the 1700's and the adjoining **Currituck County Jail**, circa 1820, one of the oldest surviving jails in the state. The current courthouse has a small brick core of pre-1869 vintage with additions from 1897 and 1952 (Bisher and Southern, 1996). These buildings are both visible from the water. Across the street from the courthouse and jail are the private **Walker House**, circa 1875, and the **General Store** from 1898. Neither is open for viewing, so admire from the road.

Former Currituck County Jailhouse

*vs*

# Coinjock Bay/Cedar Bay/ Poplar Branch Islands

Coinjock Bay and Cedar Bay are both open bodies of water with no shade and vulnerable to winds and storms. However, even if a paddling trip is not planned, a drive through the old and new quaint communities bordering the bays should be planned.

On Bell Island, most of the streets are named for the waterfowl found here during the migratory season. Most of the property is private, the views are magnificent, and at the right time of year a lot wildlife may be observed. Ducks, geese and swans can be seen flying in formation overhead during the fall and winter months and wading birds in the spring and summer.

## Location

The irregularly-shaped Coinjock Bay is located to the west of Currituck Sound, separated from it by Church Island. It is south of Tulls Bay and the North Landing River. Cedar Bay consists of two bays to the east of Coinjock Bay.

## Access Points

A.  SR 1245 /Bells Island Campground

B.  SR 1142/Waterlily Road

C.  Route 3/Poplar Branch Landing

Simmons Pond on Bells Island

*vs*

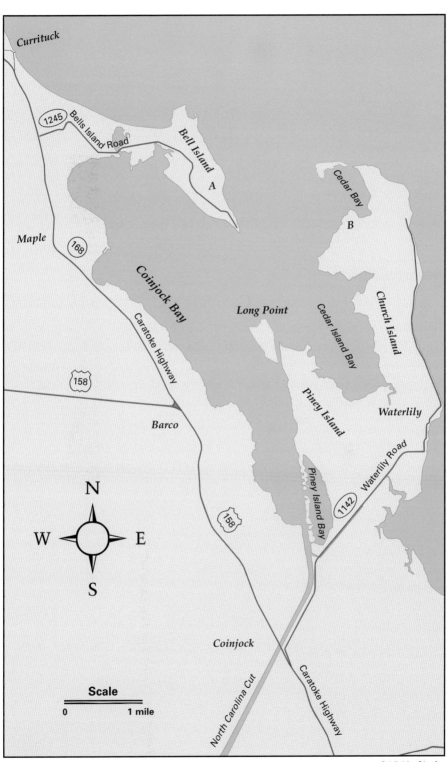

Currituck

1245
Bells Island Road

Bell Island

A

Cedar Bay

B

Maple

168

Coinjock Bay

Long Point

Cedar Island Bay

Church Island

Piney Island

Waterlily

Caratoke Highway

158

Barco

Piney Island Bay

1142

Waterlily Road

N
W E
S

Scale
0          1 mile

158

Coinjock

North Carolina Cut

Caratoke Highway

**Map 19:** Coinjock Bay to North Carolina Cut

137

© *Vickie Shufer*

Concrete ramp at Bells Island Campground on the North Landing River          *vs*

## Access Points

### *(A) SR 1245/Bells Island Campground. Currituck County*

*Directions:* From the town of Currituck, North Carolina, go south on U.S. Route 168 a little over a mile to SR 1245/Bells Island Road and turn east (left). Follow the causeway almost to the end of Bell Island. The campground is on the north at 769 Bells Island Road. Follow the road around to the office and check in with the manager to pay the boat launching fee.

*Camping:* Camping is available at the Bells Island Campground year round . There is a combination of tent sites and RV sites, with or without electricity. Rates vary accordingly. For information, call (252) 232-2716 or (252) 232-2590.

Bells Island Campground          *vs*

# Early Beginnings

1915 Ferry at Coinjock

The origin of the word, Coinjock, is from the local American Indians and is believed to mean "place of the blueberry swamps" (Currituck County Bicentennial Committee, 1976). The name has undergone several spellings throughout its history. The earliest land grants in 1683 list acreage on "Cowen Gock in Curretuck Beg. on a bay; towards mouth of Sanders Cr." (Nugent, 1977). In 1688, 2600 acres were granted to Col. Mason, Thomas Mason and Thomas Willoughby "at Corrotuck commonly called White's Island; bounded E. by Corrotuck Bay bet. The inlets of Roanoake & Curretuck, N. with Cowinjock Bay &c" (Nugent, 1977).

It is interesting to note that these land grants are both listed in the Virginia Patent Book No. 7 as being located in Lower Norfolk County of Virginia. Even though Carolina was separated from Virginia in 1663, the location of the true boundary line between the two was controversial. In 1728 a team of Virginia and North Carolina Commissioners and surveyors set the line at 36 degrees, 31 minutes beginning at the old Currituck Inlet.

In later years, the U.S. Coast and Geodetic Survey determined the boundary line, which begins at Currituck is 36 degrees, 33 minutes and 15 seconds (Boyd, 1929). Currituck Inlet has moved several times as a result of coastal storms and shifting sand. Currently, no inlet exists from Currituck Sound to the Atlantic. Coinjock Bay lies north to south on a reading of about 36 degrees, 26 minutes to about 36 degrees, 22 minutes, well to the south of the old dividing line.

At the end of Waterlily Road is Church Island, named for Richard Church, who first bought property from Timothy Ives in 1668 along a creek off the eastern branch of the Elizabeth River. By 1724, a Mr. Church had received his commission as a precinct court justice. In 1725, he was elected to the House of Commons by Currituck citizens (Pritchard, 1965).

William Byrd mentions Church and Bell Islands in his 1728 *History of the Dividing Line*. Waterlily is the home of the former 1930's **Hampton Lodge**, one of the many fishing and hunting lodges located in the area. Today the name lives on in the Hampton Family Campground, at the tip of Church Island. The causeway that leads to the end of the island, Waterlily Road, was originally a "punching road" or "corduroy road" built from logs placed side by side along the sandy soil (Trout, 1998).

# (B) SR 1142/Waterlily Road. Currituck County

*Directions:* From U.S. 158, about 10 miles east of Elizabeth City and south of Barco, follow U.S. 158 south and cross over the high rise Joseph Palmer Knapp Bridge over the Intracoastal Waterway (ICW). At the northeast side of the bridge, follow signs to Coinjock. From Coinjock, North Carolina, go south on U.S. 158 to SR 1142/Waterlily Road and turn east. Follow the causeway north and east to Church Island. Waterlily has an access site to Currituck Sound at the end of Church Island. The public boat ramp is on the west side of the road.

*Facilities*: **Midway Marina and Motel**, 157 Coinjock Development Road, Coinjock, NC 27923, (252) 453-3625. www.midwaymarina.com. This motel allows pets, is located on the waterfront along the ICW, and has a swimming pool. **Harrison's Marina** and **Crabbie's Restaurant** are nearby. The phone number is (252) 453-2631. The **Palmer Inn Bed and Breakfast** is located near Coinjock on U.S. 168 at 3861 Caratoke Highway, Barco, NC, (252) 453-6286.

*Camping*: There is a private campground at the north end of Waterlily Road, the **Hampton Lodge Camping Resort**, Coinjock, NC. Call (252) 453-2732 for more information.

Aerial view of the northern tip of Church Island;    *lg*
Hampton Lodge Camping Resort is waterfront, right near center

140

# (C) Route 3/Poplar Branch Landing, Currituck County

*Directions:* From Route 168 at Coinjock travel south 4.9 miles by vehicle to the intersection of Route 3/Macedonia Church Road. Turn east/left on Route 3 and travel 1.2 miles to Poplar Branch Road which becomes NC Route 3 at this point. In 1.1 miles, the parking area for the boat ramps is visible. There is ample parking for many vehicles with or without boat trailers.

**Caution:** The prevailing breeze is from the northeast and can make a day of paddling quite a chore. Do check the weather forecast before starting out.

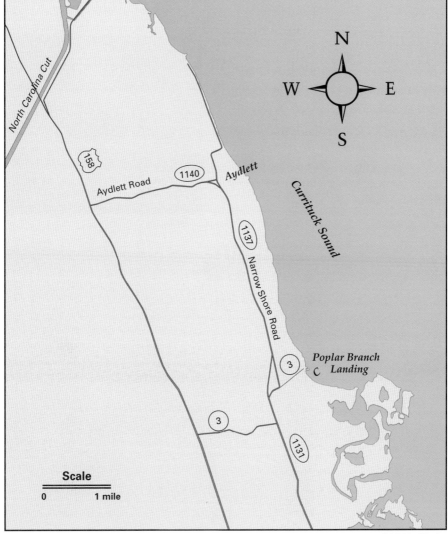

**Map 20:** Poplar Branch Islands                                                                    © Vickie Shufer

## Paddling Sections

1. SR 1245/Bells Island Campground, mileage variable

2. SR 1142/Waterlily Road, mileage variable

3. Route 3 to Poplar Branch Islands - mileage variable

### Section 1. (A) SR 1245/ Bells Island Campground, mileage variable

From Bells Island campground, paddle east to the tip of Bell Island. Go around the end of the island and into the calmer waters on the southern side. The paddler is now away from the predominant northerly breeze, which the locals say is always present.

The paddler will notice several duck blinds, an indication that waterfowl is present in the winter months. An occasional bald cypress tree can be spotted but mostly the marsh consists of black needlerush, bulltongue, rose mallow, groundsel bush, asters and goldenrod. Paddle under the bridge into Simmons Pond, ringed by wood duck nesting boxes.

Rose Mallow *vs*

Causeway Bridge on Bell Island *vs*

## Brief History of Bell Island

Bell Island is probably named for John Bell who was granted land here in the 1700's. Although the land changed owners many times the name remained the same. The Bell Island Hunt Club was established in the early 1900's. After its closing in 1938, the land was used as pasture land for cattle (Coppedge and Johnson, 1991). The bell from the Bell Island Hunt Club is on display at the Whalehead Club's landing in Corolla. Today the land is dotted with homes, the views spectacular.

## Section 2. (B) SR 1142/Waterlily Road, mileage variable

After launching at the concrete boat ramps, turn to the north into the Intracoastal Waterway (ICW). An interesting part of this journey can be a side trip into the little inlets produced by the spoil banks from dredging that has kept the channel open for commercial and pleasure boat traffic. While it would be difficult for a motorboat to navigate in these shallow inlets, a canoe or kayak can glide effortlessly here. The reward for quiet paddling is the opportunity to see a group of otters. On our last trip here, on a warm summer day, as if on cue, one would pop up, then another, then another. The water was alive with lithe chirping swimmers. One with a baby on its belly came close as did another with a shell on its belly. Our group didn't know if we were the attraction or if the otters wanted to show us what they were carrying. Their swimming agility was as athletic as it was humorous.

Exposed roots on North Carolina Cut                                                                                     lg

Former "Lighthouse"                                                                 vs

## A Lighthouse of a Sort

Paddling the course of the ICW through the cut that separates Long Point from Piney Island, the paddler will notice the old brick foundation and cistern of a lighthouse station that was active during the 1870's and beyond. The canal's section master occupied the house built here at the northern entrance to the North Carolina Cut. At night he displayed a large lantern on the roof, in effect making his dwelling a lighthouse (Brown, 1981). The two-story clapboard house has been moved to the west side of the ICW across from the **Coinjock Marina and Restaurant** and can be seen from the docks and walkway here.

Turning back to the ICW/Coinjock Bay at the northern end of this side trip, it is advisable for paddlers to stay close to the shoreline to avoid the larger boat traffic in the channel. The land on the east side of the ICW is owned by the Piney Island Club, chartered in 1983 (Coppedge and Johnson, 1991). The Piney Island Club maintains 6,000 acres of property, the clubhouse being visible from the ICW. We are advised that all of the shoreline and the islands are privately held. For boaters, including paddlers, that would mean being very respectful of these property holders' rights.

144

On the east side is the lower of the two bays known as Cedar Bay. The sandy shorelines are dotted with shorebirds. Close examination of the banks of the north end of Pine Island reveals fine quality red clay.

Paddling to the backside of the more southern of the two islands that make up Cedar Island (locals say they used to be joined), a surprise is in order. The foliage looks a lot like what one would find in Florida. Dwarf palmetto is one of the predominant plants.

To the west of Cedar Bay, Mate Island, which is still listed on many current maps, is actually nonexistent, except for a lone remnant of a tree. It is said that its name came from the fact that the island was formed when the spoil was piled in this location. It became "Made" Island, which later became known as Mate Island (Morris, 2002).

North and west of the lower Cedar Bay and across from the upper Cedar Bay at the tip of Church Island is Bell Island. For the aid of navigators at night in the 1870s, Bell Island had an automatic light, a gas light, that burned without the constant maintenance of a keeper. Mackie Island, to the north also had a gas light (Brown, 1981). Church Island along whose eastern side runs the paved road to Hampton Lodge Camping Resort, is named for the Church family who owned the land here in the 1700's. Before 1900 Church Island did not have a road that connected its three mile length with the mainland (Coppedge and Johnson, 1991). All people and supplies came and went by boat. Several families of waterfowlers, farmers, and fishermen lived along the high land of the island. As many as six hunting and fishing lodges were established on Church Island and local carvers kept the clubs supplied with decoys.

The North Carolina Cut offers a unique paddling perspective                                    *lg*

# History of the North Carolina Cut

Part of the Intracoastal Waterway, the North Carolina Cut was dug by dredges during the 1850's. At the same time, the Albemarle and Chesapeake Canal was cut from the Southern Branch of the Elizabeth River to the North Landing River and was called the Virginia Cut. The North Carolina Cut was easier to dig as the soil layers were sandy. As opposed to the engineering feats of lock-building that were needed at the opening of the Virginia Cut, only a drawbridge was needed at Coinjock. The U.S. Army Corps of Engineers who took control of the Albemarle and Chesapeake (A&C) Canal in 1912 also took charge of the Coinjock Bridge. It has been replaced by a fixed high-rise bridge, known as the Joseph Palmer Knapp Bridge, named after the man who owned most of the land that is now Mackay Island National Wildlife Refuge. Mr. Knapp founded the organization that would become today's "Ducks Unlimited" and made many generous philanthropic contributions to the local and state economy to benefit the school children.

During the Civil War, when the Union forces had captured or sunk the Southern naval forces operating out of the North Carolina Sounds, the lifeline between Norfolk and North Carolina was the A&C Canal. Sensing that the Union troops might use the Canal as a backdoor to capture Southeastern Virginia, the Confederates in North Carolina decided to block the route by plugging the North Carolina Cut by sinking debris in the channel. The Union troops had a similar thought about the Confederates possibly sending forces down the North Carolina Cut. So when they arrived at the Southern end of the cut and discovered the Confederates at work blockading the channel, they themselves completed the work by sinking two schooners and burning all that remained above the water. The date was February 14, 1862, two days after all but two of the seven-ship *Mosquito Fleet*, the original freshwater navy of North Carolina, were captured or sunk at Elizabeth City.

These brave little vessels of eastern North Carolina had expended all of their ammunition trying to defend Roanoke Island on February 8 and had retreated to Elizabeth City to resupply. The two ships that did escape planned to go north on the Pasquotank from Elizabeth City along the Dismal Swamp Canal to make their way to Norfolk. The first ship, the *Beaufort*, was able to get away, but the second ship, the *Appomattox*, sadly was two inches too wide to fit into the locks at South Mills. Her crew burned her to avoid her being captured (Brown, 1981).

## Section 3. (C) Route 3 to Poplar Branch Islands – mileage variable

South of Coinjock and Adylett, North Carolina is the community of Poplar Branch. Located east and south of Poplar Branch are a series of islands, all privately owned, but interesting to travel around. Please do not trespass on private land without permission of landowners.

## Historical Economic Center

Poplar Branch was one of the centers of business for the steamers that plied the waters between Munden Point (in what is now Virginia Beach, Virginia) and the Currituck Banks, North Carolina. Since Poplar Branch was on the Currituck mainland, those living on the Currituck Banks would rely on the transport of people and products to and from this point. Poplar Branch became the main shipping point for the waterfowl that was harvested in Currituck Sound. Two regular ships that frequented the docks at Poplar Branch were the *Cygnet,* a sidewheeler that operated here as early as 1878 and the *Comet* that replaced it around 1900. By 1915, the *Comet* was no longer in service and the *Currituck* took its place. Both ships were sternwheelers. The *Currituck* remained in service until 1931 (Hanbury, 1985).

Steamboat Comet ca. 1900 at Munden Point                    *Collection of Edgar Brown*

# Currituck Inlet and Shifting Sands

The first recorded inlet into Currituck Sound is reported as opening in 1657. This is probably the same cut or inlet in the coastline of North Carolina on a map dated about 1685 and marked at 36 degrees 30 minutes. It was labeled as "Caratuck." In 1728, William Byrd records that inlet as the "old" Currituck Inlet and he describes seeing a sloop in the sound that had entered thorough the "new" Currituck Inlet. This new inlet had opened during a hurricane on September 17, 1713 (NOAA, 2001). He mentions that ships having no greater than ten-foot draft could pass through it. His group went to the old inlet, the original measuring point for the boundary line between the colonies of Virginia and North Carolina. Barely an inlet at this period in history, Byrd described it as "an Opening of not quite a Mile, which at this day is not practicable for any Vessel whatsoever. And as shallow as it now is, it continues to fill up more and more, both the Wind and Waves rolling in the Sands from the Eastern Shoals" (Byrd, 1728). The new inlet was about five miles from the old inlet and closed completely before the mid 1800's.

A report in the *Pennsylvania Gazette* from October 5, 1785 reports a violent storm that occurred in late September concerning the sloop, *Delaware*, arriving from Turk's Island having lost her mast and everything on deck. "They went ashore at Currituck, to get supplies, but the gale had been so severe there, that the sea had made a breach into the Sound and laid the country under water for two or three miles, washed away many houses, together with almost all their cattle and ground stock; many of the inhabitants were obliged to secure themselves in trees, several lives were lost, and the shore for some miles was covered with drowned cattle, household goods, &c."

Other coastal storms have opened the sound to the ocean, like Caffeys Inlet in 1790, but the cuts closed quickly. As many as twenty-six former inlets along the Outer Banks have been significant enough to have had their names included on navigational charts (Kaufman and Pilkey, 1979). Today, there are no inlets from Currituck Sound to the Atlantic Ocean.

Although the Hattaras area of North Carolina's Outer Banks is not included in this book, we cannot help but note the incredible effects that pounding water and shifting sand had during and after Hurricane Isabel on September 18, 2003. Who can say what changes future storms might bring. What is certain is that the dunes and the Outer Banks will continue to move.

# Life Along the Currituck Sound

Life for folks living near Currituck Sound was busy, difficult, and different season to season. The following information is provided by E.O. "Jack" Baum about his grandfather, Josephus Baum, 1829-1913, known as Uncle Joe from Coinjock to Point Harbor:

*Josephus Baum was tall, wide of shoulder, and wore a size 14 shoe. He was typical of successful men of his time in that he worked from dawn to dusk and often many hours into the night. Much of the work he performed was purely physical. He had four farms over on the mainland at Grandy and Poplar Branch. He hunted wildfowl for commercial market, raised cattle, sheep, and hogs for market and for family consumption. He bred wild ponies, grew corn and hay over on the beach, owned and operated a grist mill, and for many years was wreck commissioner for many miles of the Atlantic seacoast. He owned four sailing vessels, two of which were two-masters; a 'flat'; and numerous sixteen-foot 'push skiffs.' The skiffs were used by him and by the sportsmen for hunting. He and his wife added to their income by taking in summer family vacationists, many from Elizabeth City.*

*Often in the spring, cattle on the open range became bogged in the mire where the high land entered the marsh. Grandpa would attach the cow's head to his saddle pony's tail and snake her out to high land. During the winter and spring months he would soak corn in pork barrels, slice ears into short lengths, and feed the herd on the range from a cart until the new mothers could care for their offspring. When the new pony colts came along he gathered water grass from the shore and mixed hominy with it to teach the colts to eat corn.*

*He raised several acres of corn over on the beach, and he put tar on every ear when it tasseled to prevent black birds and crows from attacking*

Josephus Baum     *Courtesy of Rhonda Morris*

149

the crop. He sheared sheep with hand shears. He shipped live stock by steamer from Poplar Branch to Norfolk using his schooners and flat in delivering them to Poplar Branch. He fished for sport in the surf in September and corned a couple of barrels for winter. He tried the blubber of whales and other large fish that washed up on the beach for fish oil. He blended the fish oil with carbolic acid and tar and used the concoction as a repellant for insects on horses and cattle. He and his father extracted salt from the Atlantic Ocean water about a mile south of their home. A large vat was suspended over a pit in which a fire was maintained to evaporate the ocean water in a vat. The location still goes by the name Salthouse.

When my father was about sixteen years old, in the mid-1880's, he and Grandpa were coming home across the sound from Poplar Branch in a large sprit-rigged canoe. It was fashioned from several logs. The wind died out and my father started rowing. Grandpa took off his hat and laid his arm over the tiller. The moon came out and the sail sagged. My father, becoming tired, eased up on the oars. All was quiet and still. Grandpa nodded. A giant gray heron settled with his clammy wet feet on Grandpa's baldpate. Grandpa came up with a whoop and the wings of the heron flapping in his face. He was caught for once not working after dusk!

Courtesy of Elizabeth Hanbury from *Currituck Legacy*, 1985

Aerial view of Islands off Poplar Branch Landing                                                                *lg*

# Indiantown Creek

This is a popular canoe/kayak route that twists and turns in an easterly direction until it finally joins the North River. Bordering the north side of the creek for about half of the trip is the "North River Black Bear Sanctuary." Occasionally a fallen tree requires some maneuvering, but this is a beautiful waterway with hardwood and cypress trees all along the route. The river's headwaters are shallow and narrow. The second mile of the river opens up to about 20-35 feet wide and remains so until the bridge at SR 1147/Indiantown Road. Be observant for the local wildlife, particularly snakes. Insects can also be pests at certain times of the year.

## Location

Indiantown Creek connects the Great Swamp of North Carolina with the Great Dismal Swamp of Virginia /North Carolina by way of Run Swamp Canal. It is also the dividing line between Currituck and Camden County in eastern North Carolina.

## Access Points

A.  SR 1148/Four Forks Road

B.  SR 1147/Indiantown Road

*That moment when you ease the canoe from the bank into the current, you sense you are part of something very old and very precious.*
  *– John C. Sawhill, past President, The Nature Conservancy*

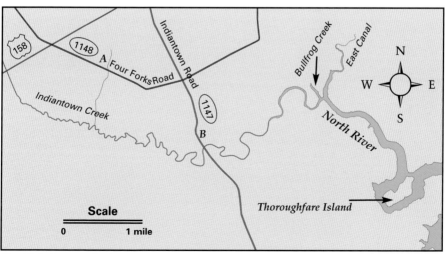

**Map 21:** Indiantown Creek

© Vickie Shufer

## Access Point
### (A) SR 1148/Four Forks Road

*Directions*: From Elizabeth City follow U.S. Route 158 east for 8½ miles. Turn southeast on SR 1148/Four Forks Road and drive less than ½ mile to the access at the side of the road where it crosses a small canal. There's only room for one or two cars. Put in on the south side at the double culverts under SR 1148, and head south. A shuttle can be done by putting in at this site and taking out at the bridge on SR 1147/Indiantown Road.

The canal drains farmland and therefore is subject to algae growth from the nutrients applied to the fields. This is not an attractive paddling location at certain times of the year, but the canal joins Indiantown Creek in less than a mile. At the confluence with shady Indiantown Creek, turn east and paddle the creek as it curves more and more until reaching the bridge on SR 1147/Indiantown Road.

### (B) SR 1147/Indiantown Road

*Directions*: From Elizabeth City, go east on U.S. 158 about 11 miles to the intersection of SR 1147/Indiantown Road and turn south (right). Go almost 4 miles until you come to a small bridge with a concrete boat ramp on the northeast side of the river. There is room for possibly ten cars, depending on everyone's geometry. Since there is no take-out point on the North River, it will be necessary to do a round trip paddle and return to the access site. Take extra time to explore this area of the county by road and be rewarded by seeing vast tracts of farmland and open fields. This is a great Sunday drive on a fall day with a variety of hawks migrating through the area.

Launch site on Indiantown Road

*vs*

## Paddling Sections

### Section 1. (A) SR 1148/ Four Forks Road to (B) SR 1147/Indiantown Road – 3 miles, one way. Currituck and Camden Counties, NC

Indiantown Creek is the boundary line between Currituck and Camden County south of U.S. 158. The man-made canal leading to Indiantown Creek from SR 1148 may be unpleasant in late summer due to possible algae growth, but it is a short trip.

The paddle trip on Indiantown Creek is a treat. We decided to nick-name this creek "Tall Cypress Knees Route," due to the most unusual collection of tall, oddly shaped cypress knees found here. The height of the knees represent how high the water level has been over the years, indicating the water level today is much lower than in past years.

Large cypress trees, many of them draped with Spanish moss, add to the uniqueness of this paddling trail. We had a wonderful day identi-fying groundnuts, swamp milk-weed, cardinal flower, spatterdock, swamp azalea and several species of

Cypress knees                                   lg

Viburnums. A barred owl was awakened as we came around the corner and great blue herons managed to stay just ahead of us. We marveled at the variety of dragonflies, and were grateful to have them, knowing they would keep the mosquito population down.

**Note:** SR 1147/Indiantown Road is an alternate put-in for this section. Paddle west from the bridge as far as time allows or until deadfall hampers paddling.

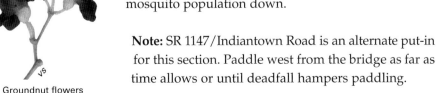

Groundnut flowers

## The Indians of Indiantown

Indiantown Creek got its name from a village of Algonquian Indians who lived near here prior to and during the early years of colonization. The Yeopim River gets its name from this group of Yeopim (Yawpim or Yeopin) Indians. These American Indians were part of a larger group who had lived, farmed, and hunted in the Pasquotank area. It is documented that shortly after 1700, the Yeopim group had been reduced to six individuals (Rights, 1957). In 1703, the Indians who lived here were assigned to a dedicated reservation of four miles square, over 10,000 acres. The tract of land was in both Camden and Currituck Counties. Court records from April 12, 1704 indicate that the "Surveyor general or Deputy shall (with what expedition is possible), upon complaint of the Yawpin Indians lay out for the sd Indians (where they now live) four square miles of land or the Quantity not injuring any of the old Settlements which was made before the order of Council bearing the date in October, 1697" (Hathaway, 1900). During the 1720's the American Indians began selling their reservation lands to settlers. By 1728, a map locates the reservation only on the Camden side. However, there have been more relics found along what is known as Indian Ridge in Currituck than have ever been found in Camden. The *Edward Mosely Map of 1733* shows a cluster of Indian homes located on the reservation land. By the 1750's, almost all of the reservation had been sold (Forehand, 1977).

## Section 2. (B) SR 1147/Indiantown Road to, and including, North River Loop – 4 miles, round trip. Currituck and Camden Counties, NC

The river at the bridge on SR 1147/Indiantown Road is inviting with its large cypress trees and summering osprey. On one trip in late April several fish were jumping and locals reported catching bass, crappie and an occassional catfish. While standing on the bank we were jumping around fighting deer flies. On a trip in early September there were no insects. At the bridge (which was built in 1937) the creek is about 25 feet wide. The ramp is paved and the river bottom sandy. This part of the creek widens as it gently flows in a meandering route to the North River.

## McKnight's Inland Shipyard

vs

It is hard to imagine now, but on the south side of the Indiantown Creek on high ground was the location of the largest inland shipyard in North Carolina. It was built by Thomas McKnight before the Revolutionary War. He was the Clerk of the Pasquotank Court before the war began. During the war, McKnight joined the British forces and was a captain with Lord Dunmore during the siege of Norfolk, Virginia (Forbes, 1953).

The distance from the bridge to the beginning of the "Loop" is about 4 miles by water. The loop is really an old oxbow in the river where a channel broke through the low wetland to create a shortcut. Oxbows are so named because they resemble the shape of the yoke worn by oxen.

The 1 mile loop around Thoroughfare Island begins about 1⁴/₁₀ mile past Bullfrog Creek. Return to the bridge at 1147. See map, page 149.

**Bonus paddling trips in this section:** If deciding to extend the paddling trip, there are two smaller swampland creeks that enter Indiantown Creek as it joins the North River. Bullfrog Creek (also called "Frog Crik") enters Indiantown Creek after 2½ miles and East Canal is the next waterway. Both are on the north side of Indiantown Creek as the paddler heads east. Bullfrog Creek is a small canopied waterway, cool and green on a hot summer's day and interesting in any season. Both of these small creeks are part of the North River Game Land, as is most of the Great Swamp to the north and east of the North River and east of Bullfrog Creek.

## Section 3. (B) SR 1147/Indiantown Road to Coinjock Bay – 14 miles, one way. Currituck and Camden Counties, NC

This paddling section begins at the same bridge mentioned in Section 2. About four miles south of the "Loop" at Thoroughfare Island, the North Carolina Cut for the Intracoastal Waterway joins the North River. The center channel is quite deep and the river is over a mile wide at this point. To reach Coinjock, paddle into Taylor Bay, going northeast into the North Carolina Cut toward the town of Coinjock, North Carolina. For more information on Coinjock Bay, see page 134.

## Section 4. (B) SR 1147/Indiantown Road to (D) Garlingtons Island Road – 9½ miles, one way. Camden County, NC

About 3½ miles south of Thoroughfare Island, look for the first opening to the west. This will lead to Crooked Creek and will take you to the asphalt boat ramp at the end of Garlingtons Island Road. Plan a shuttle if you wish to use this as your take-out.

Boat ramp on Garlingtons Island Road

*vs*

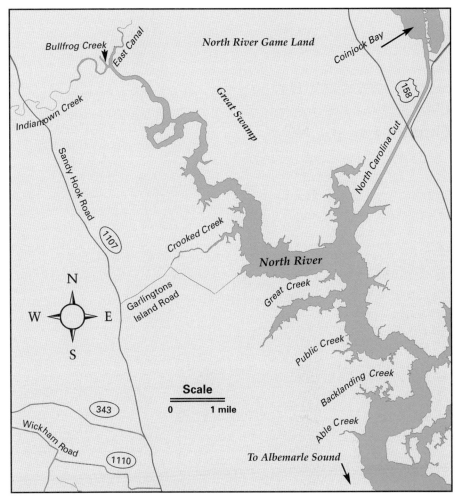

**Map 22:** Indiantown Creek to North River    © Vickie Shufer

To reach the Albemarle Sound, continue south on the North River past Great Creek. The river narrows again for another three miles before widening as the North River joins the Albemarle Sound. Total mileage from the loop to the Sound is eleven miles. This can be a treacherous trip in wind and high waves. We recommend sticking to the smaller streams, but are including this section's information for the benefit of those who like longer paddling trips.

The marsh lands of the Great Swamp border the North River for its entire length. There are small developments only at the very south end of the North River where it joins the Pasquotank. On the east side are the bear sanctuary and the North Carolina Game Land. On the west are several creeks that enter the North River, adding diversion to the larger waters of the North River. They include Great Creek, Public Creek, Backlanding Creek and Abel Creek.

157

# Part Six

# Pasquotank River

# and its tributaries

# Pasquotank River

The Pasquotank begins small and gradually widens as it flows southeasterly until its confluence with Joyce Creek near South Mills, North Carolina. Paddling on the Upper Pasquotank is delightful. There are many places where the paddler experiences total isolation, where there are no sounds except natural ones, and where wildlife finds sanctuary. Do not rule out a summer trip if the water levels are high enough to paddle. In the cool green of this water trail, we find it pleasant even when the temperatures at the put-in register near 90°.

The centerpiece of the Pasquotank is the largest city on its banks, Elizabeth City, North Carolina. The Elizabeth City Historic District contains the largest number of antebellum commercial buildings in North Carolina. The thirty-three-block district is listed in the National Register of Historic Places. Walking tours are encouraged and maps are available from the Elizabeth City Area Chamber of Commerce, McMorrine and Ehringhaus Streets, P. O. Box 426, Elizabeth City, NC 27907; or by phone, (252) 335-4365; or on the Internet at www.elizcity.com. Read more about Elizabeth City on pages 162-163.

## Location

The headwaters of the Pasquotank River begin deep in the Great Dismal Swamp, about five miles south of the Virginia line and seven miles south of Lake Drummond. It forms the curving boundary line between Pasquotank and Camden County in North Carolina for all but four miles of its length.

## Access Points

A. Off U.S. 17 near South Mills

B. SR 1211/Bingham Road

C. SR 1205/Shipyard Road

D. NC Wildlife Resources Commission Boat Ramp on Route 343

E. Elizabeth City – Waterfront Park, Dogg Corner Park, Charles Creek Park

*A river seems a magic thing, a magic, moving, living part of the very earth itself ...*

*– Laura Gilpin, 1949*

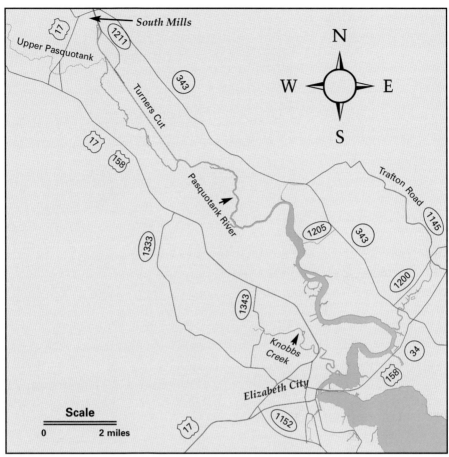

**Map 23:** The Pasquotank River from South Mills to Elizabeth City, NC © *Vickie Shufer*

Pasquotank River looking toward Elizabeth City *vs*

## Access Points
### (A) U.S. 17

*Directions:* From South Mills, turn west on Business U.S. 17/Main Street. Go to U.S. 17 and turn south (left). Go almost ½ mile and turn west (right) at the next road to the right. Go about ½ mile to the bridge crossing the Pasquotank. Park on the southwest side of the bridge and put in on either the southwest or southeast side. Both banks are steep and can be slippery when wet. Watch out for poison ivy.

For a one-way trip, drive a shuttle vehicle back to the put-in site on Bingham Road. This is a short trip and if a shuttle is not possible, make this an out-and-back trip by boat.

**Note:** There is a take-out point at the Newland Drainage Canal on SR 1360/Firetower Road if paddlers want a one-way trip and desire to run a shuttle. This trip is a total of almost 2 miles from the put-in off U.S. 17 to the alternate take-out at SR 1360. To drive to this take-out point, head south from the bridge and continue to the intersection of U.S. 158. The road dead-ends. Turn northwest (right) on U.S. 158 to SR 1360 and drive ²⁄₁₀ of a mile to the bridge over the Newland Drainage Canal. At the corner just before the bridge is the Newland United Methodist Church, built in 1916. We have found that access for canoes and kayaks may be the easiest on the southwest side of the bridge. Park where legal.

Newland United Methodist Church

*vs*

## (B) SR 1211/Bingham Road

*Directions:* In South Mills, North Carolina, at the east side of the U.S. 17 bridge over the Dismal Swamp Canal, turn south on SR 1211/Joy's Creek Road. Bingham Road is a southerly continuation of SR 1211 and the name changes from Joy's Creek Road to Bingham shortly after the Joyce Creek Bridge. Put in at the informal access site on SR 1211/Bingham Road. Paddle north ⅒ of a mile on a bit of the Turner's Cut section of the Dismal Swamp Canal. Take the first creek branching off to the southwest. The paddle route will be almost parallel to the DSC for about ⅒ of a mile. This creek is a fragment of Joyce Creek that joins the Upper Pasquotank.

## (C) SR 1205/Shipyard Road

*Directions:* From South Mills, drive 9 miles south on NC Route 343 to SR 1205/Shipyard Landing Road. Turn west. The one mile road begins as a paved road and changes to a gravel road halfway to the waterfront. The road ends at the small public ramp. Parking is very limited as there are private homes on either side of the ramp. Please avoid encroaching on private land.

## (D) Route 343 - at Sawyers Creek

For driving directions for Sawyers Creek on NC Route 343, see map on page 159. Put in at the access on NC Route 343 at Sawyers Creek and paddle into Elizabeth City. The easiest take-out point is a boat ramp at Waterfront Park. To get there by water approaching Elizabeth City from the north, paddle under the U.S. 17 Bridge and along Elizabeth City's town docks and seawall. Then paddle toward the Shepard Street Bridge. There are ramps on both sides of this bridge. Shepard Street changes to Riverside Drive at the bridge.

Bridge over the Pasquotank River approaching Elizabeth City                              *vs*

163

# (E) Elizabeth City – Waterfront Park, Dogg Corner Park

*Directions:* Elizabeth City is 21 miles south of the Virginia/North Carolina state line on U.S. 17 and is on the west side of the Pasquotank River. From NC Route 168, take NC Route 34/U.S. 158 west toward Elizabeth City. Cross the bridge over the Pasquotank River and turn south (left) on Water Street, the first street past the bridge. When approaching from the west on U.S. 17, follow Business 17/Eringhaus Street east to its end at the waterfront and turn south (right). Waterfront Park is immediately on the east (left) side of the road, across the street from the Museum of the Albemarle. Dogg Corner Park is on the same side of the street as Waterfront Park beyond where the bridge crosses Charles Creek. Water Street changes its name to Southern Avenue at the intersection with Shepard Street. Access to the river is easy here and ample parking provides a good place for a walk through this charming town. On the corner is the Fish Fry Shelter, a public red brick pavilion, where periodically, charitable organizations sell meals. Charles Creek Park, on the southeast side of the Shepard Street/Riverside Drive Bridge, can also be used as an access site. It lacks the boat ramps of the other two parks, but has a low bulkheaded waterfront area. It is across the street from the College of the Albemarle Canoeing and Boating Center.

Launch site at Dogg Corner Park                                           *lg*

164

*Facilities:* Many. Elizabeth City has a large, active and historic waterfront. Water Street is the downtown street paralleling the Pasquotank River. At **Waterfront Park** there is ample parking for cars or boat trailers. Other amenities include restrooms, picnic tables and shade trees. It is an easy walk to several restaurants, shops and places of interest. Along the waterfront walk, one will encounter several historic markers. One, concerning Wilbur Wright of early aviation fame, is on Water Street between Church Street and Fearing Street. It is from this site in

**WRIGHT BROTHERS IN THE ALBEMARLE**

*I engaged passage with Israel Perry on his flat bottom schooner fishing boat, the Curlicue.*
Wilbur Wright, September 11, 1900

This was the first of many trips made by Wilbur and Orville Wright from Elizabeth City to Kitty Hawk.

Photograph courtesy of the Museum of the Albemarle. (This sign is made possible through the support from: EAGLE MART 1&2 AND THE DAILY ADVANCE)

*vs*

1900 that Wilbur hired a small boat to take him to a larger vessel waiting in the Pasquotank harbor for the trip to Kitty Hawk, North Carolina. On December 17, 1903, he and his brother, Orville, would make history with their flying machine.

The Pasquotank Indians were the earliest residents who saw Europeans as early as 1585 in this area. The nearby **Museum of the Albemarle** houses artifacts and exhibits portraying the history of the ten-county Albemarle sound region.

If time allows, visit the **Farmer's Market** for some fresh produce or some of Miss D's fried pies, home-baked breads or cakes. Local seasonal foods are a very affordable treat.

*Camping:* **Fun Junction**, located at 983 Simpson Ditch Road near Elizabeth City, has ten primitive campsites. For information, call (252) 337-6600. **Quality Inn** at 522 S. Hughes Boulevard in Elizabeth City has a campground and ten RV hook-ups. They can be reached at (252) 338-3951.

*Bed & Breakfast:* **Elizabeth City Bed and Breakfast**, 108 Fearing Street, Elizabeth City, (252) 338-2177; **Scarlett's Inn 1856**, 1937 North Road, Elizabeth City, (252) 334-9500.

*... the Eastern Emporium of North Carolina.*
– 1830's promotional information for Elizabeth City

# Paddling Sections

1. U.S. 17/Upper Pasquotank River near Morgans Corner to Great Dismal Swamp – Mileage variable.

2. U.S. 17/Upper Pasquotank River to SR 1211/Bingham Road – 2³⁄₁₀ miles.

3. SR 1211 to SR 1205 – 11³⁄₁₀ miles

4. Pasquotank River from SR 1205 to NC Wildlife Resources Commission Boat Ramp on NC Route 343 – 5⅓ miles.

5. Route 343 to Elizabeth City Waterfront Park – 4½ miles

6. Waterfront Park to Cobb Point – 2 miles

## Section 1. (A) Upper Pasquotank River to Great Dismal Swamp. Mileage variable. Pasquotank County, NC

Head west from the put-in point and be prepared for one of the most shaded of river trips. There is a slight current to this part of the Upper Pasquotank, which makes an out-and-back trip very enjoyable. Just keep track of time and decide when the comfortable return trip is warranted.

After 1⁴⁄₁₀ miles the Newland Drainage Canal enters the Pasquotank from the west. The Pasquotank twists and turns quite a bit as it makes its way deeper into the Great Dismal Swamp. From time to time along the trip, an occasional house or farm clearing is visible and an old lookout tower can be seen to the west at about the 3 mile point. After 4 miles, no houses or cleared land will be seen. On the topo map, the Pasquotank continues a natural path another 4 miles into the swamp before it becomes County Line Ditch at the

## Canoe Trail System

This route is part of the Albemarle Regional Canoe Trail System. For more information about the system of coastal paddle trails, visit www.ncsu.edu/paddle trails/albemarle, or contact the Albemarle Resource Conservation and Development Council in Edenton, NC 27932, (252) 482-7437.

ALBEMARLE REGIONAL CANOE TRAIL SYSTEM

UPPER PASQUOTANK RIVER - 18 MILES

FOR ADDITIONAL INFORMATION CALL (919) 482-7437

VS

Great Dismal Swamp National Wildlife Refuge (NWR) boundary. We have never made it that far due to deadfall. Within the Great Dismal Swamp NWR, paddling on any ditch other than the Feeder Ditch is not allowed.

## River Highlights

If you like big trees, you will enjoy this part of the Pasquotank. We nicknamed this section the "Green Giant Trail" due to the enormous bald cypress trees and large stands of the plant called lizard's tail that grow here. Loud squawking calls alerted us to the presence of great blue herons. At the same time we started noticing large nests in the tops of trees and realized we had entered a heron rookery.

### American Indian Heritage

The Pasquotank has served as a water highway and food resource for American Indians, then early explorers who ventured into the area long before permanent white settlements. Today it is still a working waterway, but also provides wonderful recreation opportunities and a rich historical legacy.

North Carolina's Pasquotank, an American Indian name for this area, means "where the currents divide." The chief of these indigenous people, which are estimated to have numbered 1,500 to 2,000 at the time of contact with the English, was Okisko, king of the Weopmick. Okisko's people occupied all of the area that became the counties of Currituck, Camden, Pasquotank, and Perquimans. Early explorers mention names of the major villages as Weapomeiok, Pasquenoke, Chepanoc, Mascoming, and Metachkwam. When offered an opportunity to join forces with another group who lived on the Chowan River to try to drive out the English, the Pasquotank chief, Okisko, refused. This notable American Indian is today remembered by a road named for him in Pasquotank County, which parallels part of the Little River not far from Elizabeth City.

The early colonists began to settle first along rivers and creeks and spread into the mainland as they claimed and cleared more and more land. By the early 1700's the American Indian towns on the Pasquotank had been reduced to one and the native residents along the Pasquotank River numbered only about 50 individuals (Rights, 1957).

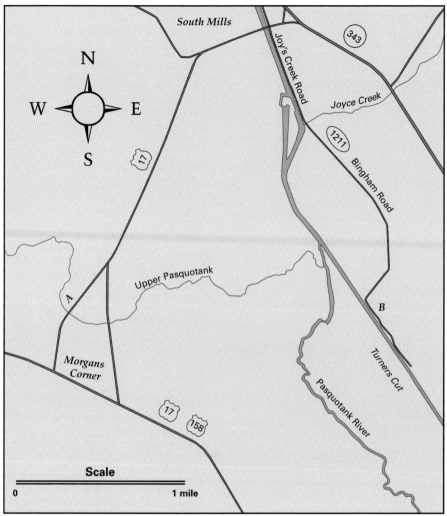

**Map 24:** Upper Pasquotank River © *Vickie Shufer*

## Section 2. (A) Upper Pasquotank River to (B) SR 1211 /Bingham Road - 2 ³/₁₀ miles. Camden and Pasquotank Counties, NC

Head east from the put-in and follow the main channel. After about 1½ miles, look for the split where the river branches off to the north and south with a mileage marker on the east side of the river. Go north for about ¹/₁₀ of a mile to the Turner's Cut section of the Dismal Swamp Canal and then go south approximately ⁴/₁₀ of a mile. The take-out is on the east side of the river at the small unpaved boat ramp. This ramp has a sandy bottom and is a very easy put-in/take-out point for canoes and kayaks.

## Section 3. (B) SR 1211/Bingham Road to (C) SR 1205/Shipyard Road –11⁴/₁₀ miles. Camden and Pasquotank Counties, NC

This part of the Pasquotank River avoids most of the Turner's Cut section of the Intracoastal Waterway (ICW). This section allows the paddler a bit of refuge from the sometimes big-boat-busy ICW as well as a more natural setting in which to paddle.

The first navigational aid marker on the Pasquotank is at Mile 36.7 (from Norfolk/Portsmouth's Mile Zero of the ICW), a point that is 4.8 miles from where the Pasquotank "officially" begins. From the south end of Turner's Cut near South Mills, North Carolina to Wade Point the Pasquotank is part of the Intracoastal Waterway. Then it widens slowly as it continues mostly east and south to Elizabeth City, North Carolina. After Elizabeth City, it widens to about 4 miles when reaching the Albemarle Sound at Wade Point, a grand total of 42 miles.

This cutoff rejoins the DSC/ICW after 4¼ miles. From this juncture, the paddler has 6¼ miles until the take-out at the end of SR 1205/Shipyard Road. Look for the waterfront home sites on the eastern shore for the take-out location. The small boat ramp is between a private pier and an adjoining lawn of the house to the north. The railroad bridge is beyond the take-out point.

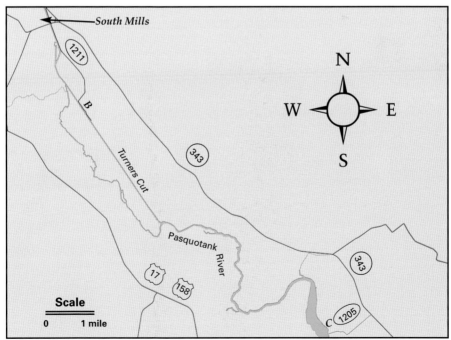

**Map 25:** Pasquotank River from South Mills to NC SR 1205    © Vickie Shufer

# Historic Site

The large brick home seen on the way to or from the take-out on Shipyard Road is the **Milford House**, said to be the oldest known two-story brick house in North Carolina. It is located south of the junction of Route 343 and SR 1205/Shipyard Road. Also referred to as the Relfe-Grice-Sawyer House, Milford was probably built by Thomas Relfe who was granted land here. An interior third floor chimney brick dated 1746 coincides with dendrochronology findings which date the last year of tree growth rings to be 1744. Allowing for a two year construction period, the dated brick probably indicates the completion year. In 1972, the **Milford House** was placed on the National Register of Historic Places. Its Flemish bond brickwork with glazed headers is reminiscent of colonial construction in Williamsburg, Virginia, but its plastered cove cornices are unusual in colonial architecture found south of Maryland or Delaware. Originally the back of the house was the front and the road to the put-in did not exist. It is a private residence today and in the past has had as owners a number of wealthy planters including Relfe, Col. Henry Palin, Joseph Jones, William Pritchard, and Pritchard's daughter, Ellen, who married John Sawyer (Forbes, 1953). The old family cemetery is on the opposite side of the road from the house. Please remember that the house and surrounding land are private property.

Milford House

*vs*

## Section 4. (C) SR 1205/Shipyard Road to (D) Route 343 at the NC Wildlife Resources Commission Boat Ramp – 5⅓ miles. Camden and Pasquotank Counties, NC

This paddling trip from the small put-in point on SR 1205/Shipyard Road to the take-out point off the ICW along a small creek to the northeast, Sawyers Creek is an interesting one because it is along the natural part of the Pasquotank River. The river makes one gentle bend and in less than a mile, Goat Island comes into view. We are told that a farmer used to keep his goats here to protect them from being killed by wild animals. The paddler may encounter motorized traffic. We have observed personal watercraft and water-skiers in warm weather. The river is slowly becoming wider although it is still only about ⅕ mile wide when reaching Sawyers Creek. Turn east into the creek and look for the docks on the north side of the creek. The take-out point is a floating dock between double boat ramps. There are no restrooms at this site. Ample parking is available for vehicles and boat trailers.

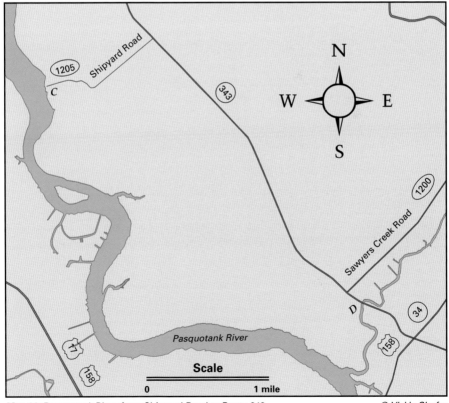

**Map 26:** Pasquotank River from Shipyard Road to Route 343          © *Vickie Shufer*

## Section 5. (D) Route 343 to Pasquotank River /ICW to (E) Elizabeth City Waterfront Park - 4½ miles, one way. Camden and Pasquotank Counties, NC.

This short paddling trip could be interrupted by personal watercraft and other motorized craft. This is a popular spot on the river. There are several private marinas, but we think it's more fun to paddle directly into town. Intracoastal Waterway mile marker 50 is at Sykes Cut just north of the city wharf. The wharf is next to Waterfront Park which is a good place to stop for a walk through this charming town.

## Section 6. (E) Waterfront Park to Cobb Point – 2 miles, one way. Pasquotank County, NC

Paddle north from Waterfront Park, past downtown and into the Pasquotank. Turn to the southeast and paddle along the shoreline. There are several piers into the waterway on this side, but on the opposite shore mostly stands of cypress and marshland. The long view down the Pasquotank is very picturesque. After passing Cottage Point, the paddler is in Forbes Bay, tucked in behind Cobb Point. At Forbes Bay, the Pasquotank is over a mile wide. This

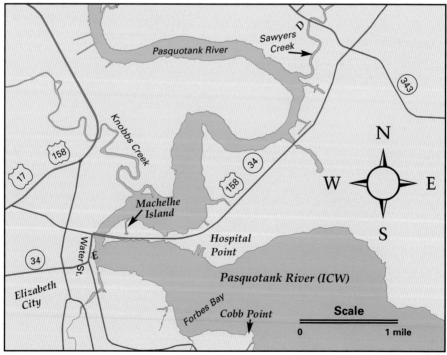

**Map 27:** NC Wildlife Resources Commission Boat Ramp to Elizabeth City      © Vickie Shufer

section of the river is protected from most threatening winds and is a favorite harbor for sailboats. Elizabeth City is home to the Moth Sailboat, first built here in 1929.

The lower portion of the Pasquotank is from 2 to almost 4 miles wide. There can be some strong winds and heavy waves on the river, making travel by canoe or kayak risky. In fact, the prevailing winds were utilized in the late 1700's by several windmills, which were built on the eastern shoreline of the Pasquotank. There were five located along the shore north of Texaco Beach. Milltown Road exists today as a reminder of their existence. One was south of Tommy's Point at the end of what is now One Mill Road (Pugh, 1953).

There is a lot of coastline to explore from Elizabeth City to Wade Point on the west side and on the east side from Hospital Point across from Elizabeth City to North River Point on the Albemarle Sound. We are not including long trips on the lower Pasquotank due to the dangers associated with open water paddling. Experienced paddlers have a lot of water to explore on the Lower Pasquotank.

Looking south towards Cobbs Point                                    lg

## Hospital Point

During the early 1800's, any seafaring village feared the visitation of foreigners who might spread contagious diseases. Cholera and smallpox were the two most feared. Health officials from Elizabeth City confined persons displaying symptoms in an isolation building outside of town. On the eastern side of the Pasquotank, the afflicted were placed in a building near the river and the place became known as **Hospital Point** (Pugh and Williams, 1964). Today's topo quads and marine charts still refer to the point of land across the Pasquotank east of Elizabeth City as **Hospital Point**.

## Steamboats to and from Elizabeth City

During the heyday of the Dismal Swamp Canal's use, steamers regularly made the one day run from Norfolk to Elizabeth City. Meals were served aboard some of the ships. The packet steamer, appropriately named *Elizabeth City*, was built especially for this trip and began its runs in 1868. The steamers would travel to Elizabeth City where

Old cobblestone street and warehouse      *lg*

passengers would spend the night and return to Norfolk the next day. Commercial ships (until the A&C Canal purchase by the federal government slowed traffic) were regularly traveling the Dismal Swamp Canal and they too would usually have a stopover in Elizabeth City. Commercial cargo from logs and timber products to watermelons and bacon all passed by the wharves and warehouses on Elizabeth City's waterfront.

One interesting and unfortunate event occurred at Woodley's Wharf on April 15, 1918 as the freight steamer, *Annie* was about to be unloaded. Her boiler apparently did not have enough water and it exploded at 9 A.M., killing five of the crewmen. One man was blown to the top of a nearby building, miraculously unharmed. *Annie* had been carrying a large cargo of groceries and many bags of flour and sugar exploded along with the boat, covering the waterfront with the look of a winter snowstorm (Brown, 1970). While there are no remains of this unfortunate mishap, many of the old warehouses remain and there are still cobblestone streets that are revealed in some asphalt-free spots near the waterfront warehouses.

## Culpeper's Rebellion

In December 1677, after a series of events affecting the political discontent of the settlers in this area, a British Collector of Customs was detained at gunpoint aboard the ship, *Carolina*, situated between Forbes Bay and Cobb Point. This and several other actions began the process of change for the settlers. John Culpeper's name may have been given to this uprising as his name most frequently appeared on the affidavits drawn up against the dissenters, or because the others involved wanted to keep a lower profile. The other settlers who were principals in the rebellion will be recognized for their names which survive today as historical figures, place-names, or localities in North Carolina and Virginia: George Durant, John Jenkins, Thomas Jarvis, John Willoughby, Patrick White, Valentine Bird, Richard Foster and James Blount (Rankin, 1962).

## The Narrows of the Pasquotank and the Founding of Elizabeth City

The part of the Pasquotank which passes by Machelhe Island, has been referred to as The Narrows at least since 1764 when the settlement was designated by law as an inspection station for products being imported or exported. Before Elizabeth City was founded, a small settlement was built at The Narrows and this was a changing station for horses on the Princess Anne, Virginia to Chowan stagecoach route. A plantation home on Knobbs Creek which was also known as "The Narrows" was inherited by Elizabeth Tooley. The daughter of early settlers, she married Adam Tooley from Princess Anne in Virginia. Among other properties, Adam and Elizabeth Tooley owned one of the few taverns in the area. The town chartered in 1793 that became Elizabeth City may have derived its name from Elizabeth Tooley who deeded to Commissioners land for the establishment of the town. In 1794, the town of Reding or Redding was established. A year later this town's name was changed to Elizabeth Town and in 1801, Elizabeth City.

Narrows of the Pasquotank

*lg*

# Protecting The Waterways For Commerce, Pre 1900's

Elizabeth City and other early towns situated around Albemarle Sound were dependent upon the waterways for transportation of products into and out of the area. With the completion of the Dismal Swamp Canal, it was possible to ship goods directly from Elizabeth City to the port of Norfolk. This had a significant effect on the local economy, but there were persistent problems with the shallow waters.

North Carolina was not blessed with deepwater ports, as were other parts of the East Coast. With the passages through the Sounds being fairly shallow and the shifting sands of the Outer Banks causing inlets to open and close, the citizens were justly concerned. To protect its port and the flow of commerce, the citizens of Elizabeth City were active in requesting help from the government. Two examples follow: In 1826 a government light ship was placed at the mouth of the Pasquotank River, signaling ships to avoid the shoals of Wade Point.

Another idea came about a year later. In the January 3, 1828 newspaper, *The American Beacon* and *Norfolk and Portsmouth Daily Advertiser*, was the following: "At a meeting of the citizens of Elizabeth City, North Carolina, on the 28th Dec., 1827. To take into consideration the best means of effecting the improvement of the navigation of the Swash at Ocracoke and likewise the opening of an inlet at the foot of Albemarle Sound by means of stopping (partially) the passage of water of Albemarle Sound through Croatan and Roanoke Sounds into Pamlico Sound" (Pugh and Williams, 1964). A committee of five was appointed to draft a petition to both Houses of Congress to deal with the proposal. The committee acted quickly and the next day prepared the information that was unanimously adopted by the citizenry. There was a noble attempt to dig out the inlet, but to no avail.

Two hurricanes changed everything. In 1828, on the coast and to the north of Elizabeth City, New Currituck Inlet closed for good, but two other inlets opened in 1846: Oregon Inlet and Hatteras Inlet. Currituck Sound as well as Back Bay in Princess Anne County, Virginia were devastated by now being largely freshwater lakes, losing profitable oyster and fishing opportunities. The Albemarle Sound did not suffer as much, being larger and with greater river drainage, but the shallow waterways have kept its ports small. The hope of becoming a major shipping area never materialized. These are nevertheless beautiful waterways with excellent recreational potential.

# Joyce Creek

Joyce Creek is a joy to paddle. It can be paddled into the Dismal Swamp Canal (DSC) to the west or to the east for a longer trip. East of the DSC, it begins as a narrow creek, about twenty feet wide and broadens only a little along its course. The creek has been cleaned and dredged although there are not high spoil banks and very little debris. Paddling with a group is easy because of the gentle meandering of the creek and the fairly consistent width for almost its entire length. It is treed to the water on one side and the opposite side is trimmed back about ten to fifteen feet from the creek. The trees have been removed allowing the grasses, small shrubs and flowering plants a chance to flourish. Thickets of native plants provide excellent opportunities to observe the stages of forest succession.

## Location

Joyce Creek is an eastern tributary of the Pasquotank River located in South Mills, North Carolina, a town originally called Old Lebanon. Joyce Creek is a meandering stream, a short stretch of which was part of the original Dismal Swamp Canal.

## Access Points

A. **SR 1211/Joy's Creek Road**

B. **Route 343**

C. **SR 1224/Old Swamp Road**

D. **SR 1235/Carolina Road**

E. **SR 1224/Old Swamp Road (near Tar Corner)**

Paddling on Joyce Creek

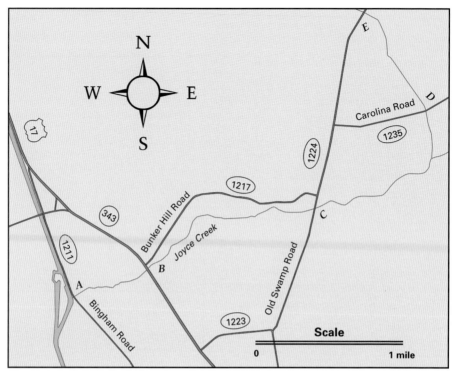

**Map 28:** Joyce Creek            *© Vickie Shufer*

## Access Points

**Note:** While all of these sites are easily accessible, they are so close together that we have only chosen to use two of them in the Joyce Creek paddling section (near Tar Corner).

## (A) SR 1211/Joy's Creek Road

*Directions:* From South Mills, North Carolina at the east side of the U.S. Business 17 Bridge across the Dismal Swamp Canal, SR 1211/Joy's Creek Road is the first turn to the south. The bridge over Joyce Creek is just over a mile from the U.S. 17 bridge. There is easy parking for many cars on any side of the bridge.

The informal access for Joyce Creek is on the east side of SR 1211/Joy's Creek Road. The best put-in site for canoes and kayaks seems to be the southeast side of SR 1211. Watch out for poison ivy along the bank as you lower your boat to the water's edge.

## (B) Route 343

*Directions:* NC Route 343 is east of South Mills and is easily reached by either returning to South Mills and driving east to the intersection of U.S. Business

17 and NC Route 343 or continuing south on SR 1211 and turning east on SR 1212/River Bridge Road to NC Route 343. This alternate access site is listed for convenience of the paddler in case there are no parking spots available on Joy's Creek Road.

## *(C) SR 1224/Old Swamp Road (at Pierceville)*

*Directions:* From South Mills, head south on SR 1211/Joy's Creek Road about 1⁴⁄₁₀ miles, just past Antioch Church, and turn east on SR 1212/River Bridge Road. After almost ½ mile, go across the intersection of NC Route 343. At this point SR 1212 becomes SR 1223/Old Swamp Road. After ½ mile (at Johnson's Corner), Old Swamp Road turns north and is now SR 1224. Continue north on Old Swamp Road for ⁸⁄₁₀ mile to the bridge that crosses Joyce Creek. Park on either side of the bridge. This is an easy spot to park and launch or take out. A landmark is the McBride United Methodist Church, established in 1784, which is less than ¹⁄₁₀ of a mile south of the river.

## *(D) SR 1235/Carolina Road*

*Directions:* Follow the directions from above (SR 1224/Old Swamp Road to Pierceville) and continue north on SR 1224 to Carolina Road/SR 1235. Turn to the east and drive about 6⁄10 mile until the bridge over Joyce Creek comes into view. This is a good access site for a group as there is plenty of parking and boats can be launched from any side of the bridge. We recommend parking on any side except the northeast.

## *(E) SR 1224/Old Swamp Road (near Tar Corner)*

*Directions:* Follow the directions above to Carolina Road and continue north on SR 1224/Old Swamp Road about ¾ mile. Parking and boating access is easiest on the northeast side of the creek.

---

### *Historical Houses*

In and near South Mills are several older homes: the early nineteenth century **Baxter-Mullen House**, a Federal style dwelling east of the canal and north of the drawbridge; the mid-nineteenth century **Ferebee House** on the eastern bank, south of the bridge; and the **Dr. Mullen House** on Joy's Creek Road, facing the canal. Nearby is the **Abbott House**, built in the 1840's by William Riley Abbott. It was built in the Greek Revival style and is unusually large. The Abbott House was officially listed in the National Register of Historic Places in 1978. All of the houses mentioned are private residences.

---

# History

Joyce Creek, originally "Joy's Creek," was named for the patentee, William Joy, who received 640 acres of land at the confluence of the Pasquotank and Joyce Creek in 1714 (Pugh, 1953). By 1716 William Joy had acquired close to a thousand acres between the creek and the upper part of the Pasquotank River. This area was known as Joy's Fork for more than a hundred years after William Joy's death in December, 1725. By 1733, Joy's widow had sold all the family's land holdings and moved to Virginia (Pugh, 1957).

Part of this pleasant creek was formerly known as the Old Moccasin Track. As part of the original Intracoastal Waterway, Joyce Creek twisted so much that it caused slowdowns of the boat traffic on the Dismal Swamp Canal. It was determined that a "cut" should be made through the surrounding swampland to straighten the passageway. Turner's Cut, named for D. J. Turner, the contractor who dug the four-mile channel, was completed in 1856. The entrance to Turner's Cut is at Mile 33.1 from Norfolk/Portsmouth's harbor which is Mile Zero of the Intracoastal Waterway.

Six years later on April 19, 1862 a group of Confederate troops three miles below the South Mills Locks did battle with a 3,000 man unit of Union troops who had intended to destroy the locks. Using a smoke screen by burning fence posts and whatever else they could find, the Confederates opened fire when they detected that the Union soldiers were near. With the fence and other debris along Sawyer Ditch ablaze, the Confederates had hidden in another ditch 300 yards beyond. Even with the obscuring smoke, the ditch and nearby woods for cover, the shots rang out for several hours. Both sides were no doubt exhausted. Had the Union troops not withdrawn, the intended damage to the locks would have stopped any water transport on the Dismal Swamp Canal. History remembers this as the "Battle of South Mills," which the locals refer to as the "Battle of Sawyers Lane" and the Union forces at the time recorded as the "Battle of Camden." Nearby is the house built by William Riley Abbott which was used as a hospital for the wounded Confederate troops from this battle. Even though many men were wounded and many died, the victory was short-lived. It was only one month later in May, 1862, that Norfolk surrendered and the entire Dismal Swamp Canal became Union property.

## South Mills Village

About ten miles from South Mills near Juniper Run, is the location of a former millpond built about 250 years ago. Its miller was Leavin Rhodes. The area around this mill was called "Old Lebanon," named for the abundant cedar trees. The village of South Mills developed early in the nineteenth century and was originally known as "New Lebanon." The town was renamed by 1839 for the two water-powered mills that David Pritchard is said to have built south of the old locks (Forbes, 1953); hence, the "south mills." South Mills is the last of the landings or villages that developed specifically as a loading area for the transport of goods along the Dismal Swamp Canal. The old locks here were rebuilt in 1941. These locks are the ones in use today and measure 300 feet long by 52 feet wide. The floor of the lock is concrete and the sides, steel.

Joyce Creek with downed trees                                              vs

**Note:** Be aware that with the high water table of these waterways, trees may have fallen as a result of storms and high winds. We paddled most of these creeks and rivers before Hurricane Isabel of September, 2003 and acknowledge that many of these waterways may have suffered severe damage from uprooted trees. It is advisable to carry hand saws or clippers in your boat.

## Paddling Sections

1. (A) SR 1211/Joy's Creek Road to (C) SR 1224 (at Pierceville) - 1 ⁹⁄₁₀ miles

2. (C) SR 1224 (at Pierceville) to (E) SR 1224 (near Tar Corner) - 1 ⁸⁄₁₀ mile

### Section 1. (A) SR 1211/ Joy's Creek Road to (C) SR 1224 (at Pierceville) – 1 ⁹⁄₁₀ miles, one way. Camden County, NC

From the bridge on SR 1211/Joy's Creek Road looking east, it appears that Joyce Creek is immediately obstructed by brush or downed trees. This is an illusion that becomes apparent as the creek makes a turn to the south. Once away from the road there is little noise except bird sounds. Shortly after the put-in, notice that the north bank has been partially cleared in a ten to fifteen foot swath parallel to the river. The south bank is natural. After crossing under the bridge at NC Route 343, a few houses are visible, but the creek is still well populated with birds.

### Section 2. (C) SR 1224 (at Pierceville) to (E) SR 1224 (near Tar Corner) – 1 ⁸⁄₁₀ mile. Camden County, NC

While neither of these sections is a very long trip, they can easily be combined for an easy half-day paddle trip. The scenery is comparable in both sections with patches of cypress and a variety of young trees and shrubs. Glimpses of the farming community are visible in places along the route. Sometimes getting to some of the paddling sections in this book are as enjoyable as the canoe or kayak trip. It gives one a break from city life to take a drive into the country on the small back roads to a paddling adventure.

### River Highlights

We referred to Joyce Creek as "The Wild Berry Trail" during a summer of paddling because of all of the varieties of edible berries growing along one of the banks. We found blackberries, elderberries and muscadine grapes that ripened at different times in the growing season. These berries are valuable food sources for many animals and birds that rely on them.

Elderberry                                    *vs*

## Swamp Cyrilla

Nearing its northern range and fairly rare is the swamp cyrilla, also known as leatherwood or "titi." It is also native in the West Indies and from Central America to Brazil. Bees forage on the flowers for nectar to make a dark honey.

vs

## *Preventive First Aid*

Growing along the banks, in wet areas around trees, almost every river has an abundance of poison ivy. "Leaves of three, let it be," is good advice. Unfortunately, it keeps many people from enjoying the outdoors. But there is a plant that many believe provides the antidote to the contact dermatitis received from poison ivy, and that is jewelweed, a native impatiens. And while some believe it grows next to poison ivy, that's not always the case. However, it does like wet banks and the edges of streams. If you know you are allergic to poison ivy, or even if you think you're not, look for jewelweed in summer when it has orange flowers on a fleshy, succulent stem. Pick a few of the leaves, crush them up until juicy and rub on exposed areas that may have come in contact with poison ivy. It won't hurt you, and who knows, it might help.

Poison Ivy                     vs

Jewelweed                      vs

## Wildlife

We had a number of wildlife sightings while paddling on Joyce Creek. It was in the first section that we spotted a white-tail deer fleeing into the underbrush. Turtles were seen sunning themselves on logs and the bald eagle took flight as we came around a corner. There were many varieties of dragonflies and butterflies in flight over the water.

# Sawyers Creek

This blackwater creek allows access to the Pasquotank River or the upper part of the creek that drains from farmland carved from the Great Dismal Swamp. This small historic creek is easy to paddle and in the upper stretches is host to a wide variety of plants and animals. Road noise is prevalent only until after the first turn. The scenery is interesting with something different at every turn. If the water level allows, paddle beyond the take-out bridge at SR 1200/Sawyers Creek Road. The western branch of the upper creek extends several miles into the old swampland.

## Location

This small creek is located near the town of Camden in Camden County, North Carolina. Its headwaters are in the southeastern part of the Great Dismal Swamp. Sawyers Creek is an eastern tributary of the Pasquotank about three miles east and north of Elizabeth City.

## Access Point

A.  Route 343
B.  SR 1200/Sawyers Creek Rd

North Carolina Wildlife Resources Commission Boat Ramp

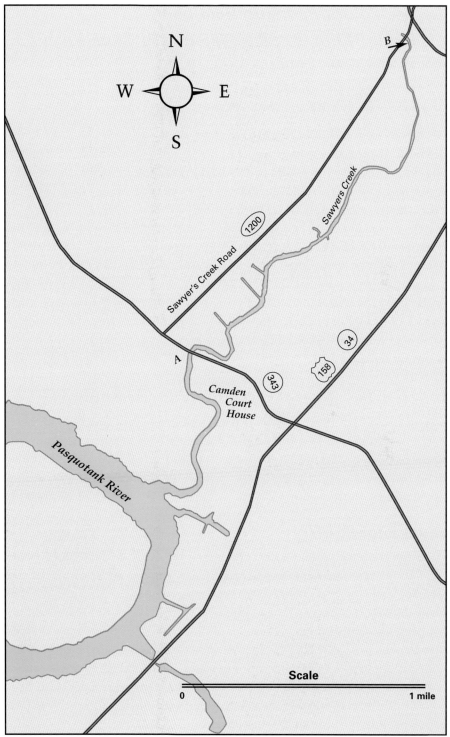

**Map 29:** Sawyers Creek

© *Vickie Shufer*

## Access Points/Paddling Sections

## (A) Route 343 to (B) SR 1200/Sawyers Creek Road - 3 miles, one way. Camden County, NC

This creek can be paddled using either road as a put-in or take-out. We're beginning at the North Carolina Wildlife Resources Commission Boat Ramp.

*Directions:* From U.S. 158, almost 1½ miles east of Elizabeth City, take Route 343 north approximately ⅒ of a mile to the Camden Community Park on the west side of Route 343. There are 13 trailer/car-parking places, 6 car-only spots and one large handicap-designated parking place. Two concrete boat ramps are separated by a floating dock.

By canoe or kayak, paddle west ⁶⁄₁₀ mile from the ramp to see the Pasquotank River. The easterly trip on Sawyers Creek begins at the widest part of this small creek, about 45 feet wide. After passing under the Route 343 bridge, the creek parallels the highway for a short distance. After the first bend, the road noises quickly disappear, to be replaced by the more pleasant sounds of cicadas or crickets. The further one paddles up the creek, the fewer fishermen there are. Allow time for exploration into a couple of the creeks along the route.

## (B) SR 1200/Sawyers Creek Road to (A) Route 343

*Directions:* To drive to the take-out on SR 1200/Sawyers Creek Road, head northwest from the North Carolina Wildlife Commission Boat Ramp on Route 343 about ⅕ mile and turn northeast (right) on SR 1200. Drive 1½ miles to the bridge crossing Sawyers Creek. Park on the northeast or southeast side of the bridge. The put-in (or take-out) is on the southeast side of the road.

## River Highlights

Swamp blackgum and bald cypress line the creek on both sides. Some spanish moss can be seen where Sawyers Creek empties into the Pasquotank. Heading east, after passing the first bend, road noise diminishes and wildlife increases. Wood ducks can be spotted in the spring with the mother duck and her babies disappearing into the cover of the swamp. Turtles sunning on logs dive into the water at the first sign of an approaching visitor and prothonotary warblers fly back and forth across the water. Yellow-billed cuckoos can be heard making a rapid "ka-ka-ka" call. Great blue herons are among the fish-eating birds that feed in these waters which are reported by fishermen to have bass, long nosed gar, catfish, crappie, bream and striped bass.

Sawyers Creek has two interesting side trips that await the adventure-some paddler. Two small creeks off to the northwest and southeast are both interesting with a wide array of plants not seen on the main part of the creek. Pickerelweed, rose mallow and sundrops are among the flowering plants. Royal ferns added a lush green color to the understory along with a number of flowering shrubs such as Viburnums, swamp roses, chokeberry and buttonbush. Wild yam, muscadine grape and groundnuts are among the vining plants growing here.

Royal Fern                                      vs

## Yellow Pond Lily

Floating on the surface of the dark waters of northeastern North Carolina are numerous colonies of plants with heart-shaped leaves and globules of yellow flowers up to 2 inches wide. Yellow pond lily, also known as spatterdock, is a member of the water lily family and a native wetland plant that makes an attractive appearance. The seeds are a food source for wood ducks and mallards.

## Ferns

Ferns are among the oldest living plants and have been around since before the dinosaurs. They reproduce by spores which either fall to the ground or are airborne. The inflorescence-like top of the royal fern consists of hundreds of small sporangia. With moisture and light, these single-celled organisms start to grow, dividing and redividing. Royal ferns spread very slowly, eventurally forming a ring around the central plant. They require acidic, very wet soil for best growth and can live in open shade or in sunlight.

Yellow Pond Lily                                vs

187

# History

Sawyers Creek is named after the landholder, Caleb Sawyer, who served as one of the representatives from the Pasquotank Precinct in the House of Commons from 1735 to 1743. At the time, Camden County had not been formed from the larger Albemarle County. In 1670 the County of Albemarle was divided into four precincts: Pasquotank, Currituck, Chowan, and Perquimans. Mr. Sawyer sponsored several pieces of legislation, one which was intended to form a separate precinct from the land on the northeast side of the Pasquotank River. With the courthouse on the opposite side at Newbegun Creek, anyone needing to do business there had to cross by ferry or other water transport. Sawyer's Ferry was fifteen miles from the courthouse and transportation by water was, at times, very dangerous. For political reasons, Governor Johnston vetoed the bill.

Because so much travel was by water rather than by the crude roads, Sawyer later proposed "An act appropriating the Powder Money towards the fortifying beaconing and Bouying out the several Ports or Channels in the province and for Imploying Pilotes" (Pugh, 1957). Waterways were indeed the preferred mode of transport.

By 1790, Sawyers Creek was a port of entry for northeastern North Carolina at "Plank Bridge" or Camden as the area came to be known. George Washington appointed its first customs collector and the port on Sawyer's Creek was a busy place for about one hundred years.

After the Revolutionary War, former Pasquotank Senator Joseph Jones, whose home was about 100 yards from the courthouse, attempted to begin a town here called Jonesboro. A lot of building was occurring nationwide. Lumber and shingles that were processed and ready for shipment from North Carolina were in high demand. The settlement had its streets platted out as is evidenced by early deeds, and by 1802 even had a post office. The development of Jonesboro did not last and the post office eventually moved to Camden. Joseph Jones is better remembered as the gentleman who introduced legislation that led to the formation of Camden County.

There were many wharves and warehouses along the creek, but the years of prosperity ended when larger, deep draft ships were constructed. Sawyers Creek could not accommodate the bigger ships and by 1830, the port of entry was moved to Elizabeth City. The only remains of the former maritime center at Plank Bridge on Sawyers Creek are some old pier timbers that can still be seen at certain water levels.

# Historic Road/Buildings

Part of today's NC Route 343 is built on the original route of the old stage coach road that led from Elizabeth City to Camden to Norfolk along the eastern edge of the Great Dismal Swamp. (Pugh, 1953). It is very likely that the southern part of this high ground

Former jail                                    vs

was originally an American Indian trail. An interesting side trip is to drive just a short distance south on Route 343 from the boat ramps on Sawyers Creek to the site of the Camden County municipal buildings. (see p. 183). The Camden County Heritage Museum is located in the former jail, built in 1910 and restored in 1986. Call (252) 338-1919 for information. An interesting historic site is the **Camden Masonic Lodge**, begun in 1820 for Widow's Sons #75, and completed as a Masonic Lodge in 1856.

The brick Camden County Courthouse was built in 1847 and replaced the original wooden building constructed in 1782. It is built in the Greek Revival style and has a portico of four large wooden columns built on story-high brick supports. The Camden County Courthouse was added to the National Register of Historic Places in 1972 and the former Jail was added to the Register in 1984.

Camden County Courthouse                                    vs

# Nearby Waterfront Nature Trail

Behind the Museum and Courthouse complex, and near the Camden County Senior Center, is a wooden boardwalk nature trail that was funded through the Coastal Area Management Act (CAMA) . The boardwalk trail leads through a forested swamp for a short distance to a waterfront gazebo looking out at Sawyers Creek. There are trashcans along the way and benches donated by the local 4-H group. Pileated woodpeckers make their presence known by the loud laughing call. They feed on the insects of old and dying trees. Red maple, ash and swamp blackgum are among the trees that grow here. In the understory, swamp roses and waxmyrtles are abundant, another food source for wildlife. While not a boating access site, this walkway is a perfect way to do some birding or to just enjoy a leisurely afternoon by the water.

Waterfront Nature Trail with gazebo in background                    *lg*

# Knobbs Creek

Knobb's Creek is what we would describe as the "Industrial Creek." At the confluence with the Pasquotank is the Knobbs Creek Deepwater Barge Site. Approximately 12 acres in size , it is a privately owned piece of prime commercial/industrial property. After a couple of bends in the creek the Commercial Ready Mix Products, Inc. site comes into view. Mounds of sand and gravel stand ready to be made into concrete. Beyond that are the remains of a dock that may have been a former sawmill. Even with the commercial development, there are still a number of natural sights to see. Unfortunately, there is no access to the upper, undeveloped part of the creek.

## Location

Knobbs Creek is located on the west side of the Pasquotank River, less than a mile northeast of Elizabeth City. Winding its way out of farmlands drained from the Great Dismal Swamp, Knobb's Creek is crossed immediately before entering Elizabeth City via U.S. 17 from the northeast.

## Access Points

A.  **Causeway Park on U.S. 158/34**

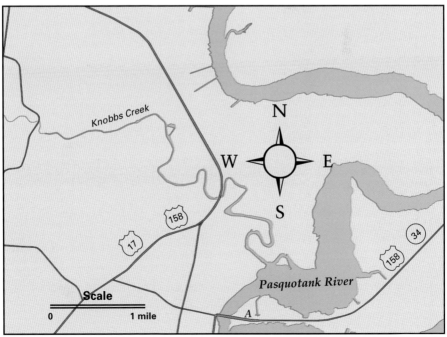

**Map 30:** Knobbs Creek

© Vickie Shufer

## Access Point/Paddling Section
## (A) U.S. 158/Route 34 at Causeway Park

*Directions:* From Elizabeth City, go east on U.S. 158/Route 34 over the bridge about ½ mile. Causeway Park is on the north side of the road with a lot of room for parking. A boardwalk trail leads to the Pasquotank River with a dock for launching a canoe or kayak. After walking a short distance, there is a fork in the trail. Both trails lead to the water's edge. While neither of the routes is very long, the shorter is to the right. It may be that the water is not deep enough to paddle from here. If so, backtrack and take the other route. There will be a dropped step to the water which makes launching and entering one's boat very easy.

vs

## Causeway Park

Causeway Park was dedicated in 1998 and was a gift to the public by a generous Elizabeth City family. The family stipulated that the property be used as a water access (Overman, 2003). The wooden boardwalk leads to the Pasquotank River. There are two picnic tables on the walkway allowing for a casual waterfront lunch. On a pleasant afternoon, several folks were observed enjoying the sunny facility while the authors were putting a canoe in the water.

Launch site at Causeway Park                                             *vs*

The paddle trips from here are three-fold. One may choose to paddle to Elizabeth City's downtown area or into the Pasquotank River to the north. The third option is to paddle northwest across the river to the protected waters of Knobbs Creek. Look for the buildings of the Roanoke Bible College and to the northeast of them in the water are the large pilings, called "dolphins." These dolphins are made of three creosote pilings bound together by heavy metal cords. You will see the opening to the right of the Knobbs Creek Deepwater Barge Site. From the river it appears to dead-end, but actually makes a sharp turn to the north. After about 1⅓ miles, a railroad crossing blocks further passage on the creek. Use this as a turn-around point.

Barge site at entrance of Knobbs Creek                                   *vs*

## River Highlights

The boardwalk trail is a good introduction to the plant life on the Pasquotank. Colonies of spatterdock, pickerelweed and lizard's tail line the walkway. Once on the river, the remains of several sunken vessels can be seen as you paddle across the Pasquotank. These form miniature islands with groundsel bush, waxmyrtle and swamp roses growing on them. There is an island is on the right just before arriving at the opening of Knobbs Creek.

Sunken vessel on the Pasquotank River                                    *vs*

Knobbs Creek makes a number of sharp turns and bends. Rather than natural vistas to greet us, there was more evidence of the industrialization that has taken place here. We did see a great blue heron, a few turtles and some wood duck nesting boxes. Red maple and sweetgum were common along the banks and were replaced with bald cypress and swamp blackgum after a short distance. Muscadine grape vines were common most of the way.

Less than a mile from the entrance is Knobbs Creek Park on the south side of the creek. There is a marked nature trail that begins on the southeast side of the park that leads through the woods to the creek and back to the parking area at Knobb's Creek Recreation Center. The park is located on East Ward Street off U.S. Business 17. The recreation center is on the east side of the street. Call (252) 335-1424 for more information.

## *History*

Very close to the confluence of Knobbs Creek and the Pasquotank River is the site of the pre-1790 former tavern, owned by Elizabeth and Adam Tooley. This waterfront establishment was probably an inn and tavern and was frequented by river travelers to the area. The plantation home inherited by Elizabeth Tooley was on Knobb's Creek.

# Areneuse/Mill Dam Creek

Areneuse Creek was formerly called "Arrownose," a description based on the look of the two prongs of the river resembling the tip (nose) of an arrow (Pugh, 1953). Originally considered the eastern branch of Areneuse Creek, Mill Dam Creek was named later for the large mill that was here and the dam built to supply its water power.

These two creeks can easily be combined to make a single trip since they connect at their southern ends where they both drain into the Pasquotank River. They are surrounded by a blend of swampland, housing, and agricultural areas.

## Location

Meandering gently out of the headwaters in what is now drained swamp lands, these two creeks terminate on the eastern side of the Pasquotank River in Camden County, east of Elizabeth City, North Carolina.

## Access Point

A. **Route 343/Areneuse Creek**

B. **Route 343/Mill Dam Creek**

Areneuse Creek

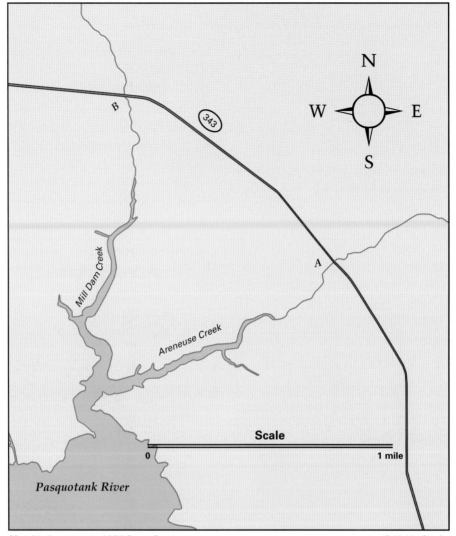

**Map 31:** Areneuse and Mill Dam Creek                    © Vickie Shufer

## *Access Points/Paddling Sections*

### *(A) Route 343 at Areneuse Creek to (B) Route 343 at Mill Dam Creek – 2 miles, one way. Camden County, NC*

Both creeks can be conveniently accessed at two bridges along Route 343 a few miles southeast of Camden. This paddling route is unusual in that two creeks can be completed in a single trip due to the V-shaped path they take in their routes to the larger Pasquotank River. We chose to use Mill Dam as the take-out because the trip can be extended inland on Mill Dam if the water is high enough.

*Directions*: To drive to these rivers from Elizabeth City, head northeast on U.S. 158 and turn southeast on Route 343 at Camden. After 3 miles, Route 343 crosses Mill Dam Creek. Park on the bridge at the concrete pullouts. There is room for two cars on each side. If running a shuttle, leave one car at Mill Dam Bridge and drive 1 ¹/₁₀ miles east to the next bridge. Park on the bridge at one of the two concrete spaces on either the north or south side of the bridge.

The easiest put-in for canoes and kayaks is on the southeast side of the creek at the low riverbank.

## River Highlights

The Areneuse begins as a narrow creek and widens after a few turns to about 35 feet. Bordering Areneuse Creek is a cypress-tupelo forest. Several wood duck nesting boxes have been placed along the river and in the small creeks feeding into the Areneuse. In late summer, crickets and cicadas drown out most road noises. Royal ferns grow in the understory as well as swamp azaleas, climbing hempweed and groundsel bush. However, the wilderness feel is too soon missed as a private community's double boat ramp and piers come into view on the north side. Houses are being built near the creek as it widens further to join Mill Dam Creek. The paddler is now at the bottom of the "V" that is formed from this duo of small creeks. Spanish moss becomes more common as you approach the Pasquotank.

Paddling due south from this junction, both creeks join the mighty Pasquotank which is two miles wide at this point. The marine chart shows a partially submerged shipwreck at the end of Areneuse Creek. The bow of the submerged boat is visible and a swamp rose bush is growing out of it. The nearby point of land is known as Treasure Point. There

Bald cypress tree covered with Spanish Moss          *lg*

is a stunning view of the big river in the distance. Looking to the northwest is a large eagle's nest. Look for the white head, sometimes seen perched on a tree branch at the water's edge. On the west side of the Pasquotank is the large steel hangar that housed lighter-than-air reconnaissance craft during World War II.

Agriculture has been Camden County's largest industry since the establishment of several plantations in the late 1600's. Today the plantations have been replaced with modern houses. Back on the partner stream, Mill Dam Creek, houses are visible until rounding a bend not far from the take-out.

If possible, extend the trip by continuing under the bridge into the headwaters of Mill Dam Creek. The narrow creek twists around large water tupelo trees. Picturesque islands have formed on tree stumps, supporting a garden of native plants. Look for rattlesnake master, cardinal flowers, pennywort and smaller forget-me-nots. Deadfall is prevalent and can easily be portaged if the water is low, although higher water will make this part of the trip easier. Mill Dam continues another mile north beyond the bridge, then splits into three very small waterways, mostly unpaddleable. Turning back to the bridge, the take-out on the southwest side of the Route 343 bridge is easiest.

Nature's landscaped garden on Mill Dam Creek                                      *lg*

# Mills and Dams

Mills are used to cut, crush, grind or provide a power source for machinery such as those that pump water in Holland. Saw mills were used in colonial North Carolina and Virginia to mill lumber into staves, boards, shingles, and uniformly cut planks and pieces for building. Grist mills were used to grind corn or other grains. These two applications require an energy source to turn the gears that do the work.

Looking at the slow-moving southern swamp creeks of the counties we studied for this book, we couldn't see that all of them could be impounded to a height enough to provide the "oomph" to turn much of anything. After all, we are almost at sea level on many of these creeks.

These water-powered mills hold some fascination when one considers what might have been the power source for turning the grindstones or the machinery. Were these tide mills, such as the ones built in England since the 1100's, or were they mills using water collected from the swampland in millponds? Did the Carolina colonists build tide mills? Was there enough tidal flow coming in through sluice gates to then be impounded and released at low tide? Was there enough depth and pressure in the impounded water to turn a large waterwheel and the machinery to grind or saw? A look at the area today suggests not, especially because these are freshwater, not saltwater creeks. There is no tide today except wind-driven tide and this would have been too unpredictable. But a look at the old geography of the area, particularly at the coastline may suggest a different answer. The area was earlier subject to some tidal influences because the ocean had several openings that do not exist any more. To say that any of the northeastern Carolina streams had enough tidal influence to be impounded for mill work is debatable, but an interesting question, nevertheless.

The only references to tide mills we have found are statements in a book by historian, Archibald Henderson. "The incoming tides had been impounded to turn the wheels of sawmills and gristmills during the colonial period, and a statute of 1715 had authorized the condemnation of sites for 'publick mills.' In spite of the topography of the coastal plain, many waterpower mills were in existence" (Henderson, 1941).

In reading about early tide mills in England, it was discovered that they were found along shallow creeks, several miles from the actual coast so as to be protected from ocean surges or troublesome waves, but still within the range of the tide. Always there were ponds behind the mill, formed by building a dike or dam across the mouth of an estuary that drained into a larger river or bay. These milldams were also utilized as roadways over the former creek openings. Along Route 343 the road crosses over at least three of these early mill sites. Today, the millponds left behind are homes to waterfowl and other creatures and are delightful places to paddle.

When the mills powered by water did not provide the necessary strength to grind, saw, or whatever the job required, windmills were employed in various locations. The miller was an important figure in any community and before the building of mills, all grinding was done by hand, as the American Indians had employed.

The property where the dam was built on Mill Dam Creek was purchased by Ezra Albertson from Christopher Williams in 1720. He then built a large mill and dam between circa 1740-1750 (Pugh, 1953). The Albertson Milldam was known as the second milldam and the first was built less than two miles away by Colonel Thomas Hunter in 1740.

After the Revolutionary War five windmills were built along the riverfront of the Pasquotank not far from these two early water mills, south of the Areneuse. The early name for the site was Mill Ford (or Mill Town) (Pugh, 1953). Steam powered mills were not in use until 1818 when the first in the state was built on the west side of Cape Fear River (Henderson, 1941).

Learn more about tide mills and windmills at these sites: www.iclei.org/efacts/tidal.htm, www.tem.nhl.nl/~smits/windmill.htm; www.tidemill.org.uk; www.lihistory.com/3/hs333a.htm; www.argonet.co.uk/users/eling.tidemill/hist.html.

# History

The earliest land grant in what would become Camden County was on September 25, 1663 to Thomas Woodward and his son Thomas Woodward, Jr. It was for 2500 acres "beginning at the head of the easternmost br. of Aranews Cr. &c. towards the head of the North River" (Nugent, 1992). The Areneuse was one of the first creeks to be settled upon probably because it is a protected waterway tucked in behind a small point of land that projects into the large Pasquotank River. Its easy access to a large body of water supported a landing for ships. This is mentioned in a 1704 piece of legislature as being on a road leading from the Indiantown Causeway to Store Landing on Areneuse Creek (Jones, 1977). By 1755, "Arranew's Creek" was listed in the General Assembly Records of North Carolina, 1754-55, Chapter III, as a port of inspection for pork, beef, rice, indigo, tar, pitch, turpentine, staves, headings, shingles, and lumber for the county of Pasquotank. Two years later on May 9, 1777, in the General Assembly of North Carolina, Joseph Jones sponsored legislation that created Camden County out of Pasquotank County.

By 1810 a tannery was located at "40 pound neck on Areneuse Creek" (Forehand, 1977). Many goods might have been shipped from here or other landings. In the 1810 census, Camden County listed as having the following:

| | |
|---|---|
| Linen, wool, and cotton wheels | 1104 |
| Manufacturing looms | 420 |
| Cloth of various kinds | 103,225 yards |
| Leather | 1,227 hides |
| Distilleries | 49 |
| Brandy | 13,126 gallons |

## Historic Sites

If driving from Sligo, North Carolina to Mill Dam and Areneuse Creeks, the **Shaw House** is located in Shawboro, ⅗₀ of a mile north of the intersection of NC Route 34 and North Indiantown Road. The Italianate Victorian house, built by William Shaw

The Twin Houses                                    vs

between 1880 and 1885, was added to the National Register of Historic Places on April 17, 1980. Also in Shawboro on the west side of NC Route 34 are the **Twin Houses**, built before 1797 by John Perkins. Built in the Federalist style, this pair of houses is joined by a central entryway. Do take a minute on the way to the river to glance at this unusual structure. The **Twin Houses** became part of the National Register of Historic Places on April 13, 1972. Both the **Shaw House** and the **Twin Houses** are private dwellings.

# Portohonk Creek

Portohonk Creek begins as a small creek, about twenty-five feet wide until close to the Pasquotank where it widens slightly. Trees on both sides of the creek give it a jungle-like feeling and provide shade most of the way. The trip is a short one but the alert paddler might be rewarded by seeing many varieties of birds and wildflowers. One of the paddlers on our last trip saw a fox running along the creek bank.

## Location

Portohonk Creek is a small tributary on the eastern side of the Pasquotank River. It is located ³⁄₁₀ of a mile east of the community of Shiloh in Camden County, NC.

## Access Point

A. SR 1111/Wickham Road

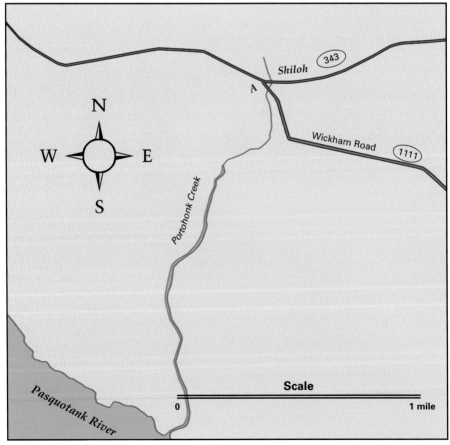

**Map 32:** Portohonk Creek

© Vickie Shufer

## Access Point/Paddling Section

## (A) SR 1111/Wickham Road to Pasquotank River - 1½ miles, one way. Camden County, NC

*Directions:* From U.S. 158, almost 1½ miles east of Elizabeth City, take Route 343 seven miles south of Camden to SR 1111/Wickham Road near Shiloh, North Carolina. Park along the road near the culverts which cross Portohonk. It may be necessary to carry the canoe or kayak a short distance through the woods on the northwest side of the creek in order to avoid deadfall. This was the case when we were last there, but the portage is short. Do watch for holes in the soft ground as the peat layers give way easily.

Portohonk Creek put-in                                                    *vs*

After putting in there is another bit of deadfall, but it is easy to push by it or over it, depending on water level. After passing a private dock, the waterway is clear of debis clogging the water trail. There are several signs on this creek placed there by the local residents. They add to the charm of this small creek. If we were nicknaming this creek, it would be "Sign Creek." Along the route, the creek is about 25 feet wide until close to the Pasquotank where it widens slightly. The trip is a short one but the alert paddler might be rewarded by seeing many varieties of birds and wildflowers.

*lg*

## River Highlights

Along the west side of the creek not far from the Pasquotank, sawgrass is present. Not really a grass, but rather a sedge, it is most abundant in the Florida Everglades. Along the opposite side is a giant stand of cattails. The edges of the creek are for the most part spotted with bald cypress near the water and pine on drier land. A lot of old, quite large stumps are a reminder of the logging heritage along these small southern creeks.

Approaching the Pasquotank, a large dirigible hangar from the 1940's is visible on the opposite shore. Read more about this on page 211. The paddler at this point is seven miles from Elizabeth City to the northwest. To paddle along the shoreline of the Pasquotank is great if the wind is not blowing. Just about a mile north of where Portohonk enters the Pasquotank were five windmills which were constructed in the late 1700's. No remnants of them remain, but if visiting on a windy day, the paddler can understand how much power was available for use by these windmills. It would perhaps be an unusual tourist attraction if these windmills could be reconstructed as a heritage park on the river.

Portohonk Creek                                                                                              vs

After paddling, drive the short distance to Shiloh and visit Midgett's General Store built in the old Shiloh High School. Enjoy a snack, ice cream, cold drinks or homemade fried pies. You'll find the folks there very friendly. There is even an ATM available if needed.

## History

Near the southern end of Camden County, Portohonk and Raymond Creek were some of the first places to be settled. The community adopted the name, "Shiloh" in about 1880, but the community's history is much older. In a land grant in the 1600's, Portohonk was called "Portabunk Creek." It is probably an Indian word whose meaning has been lost over the centuries. In 1696, a deed was recorded for John Danson of London for 3,650 acres from the mouth of Portohonk Creek along the banks of the Pasquotank to the mouth of Areneuse Creek. The sale was executed by "John Archdale Esqr Governor of North and South Carolina ... in consideration of the Sum of 36 pounds 10 shillings" (Bjorkman, 1990). Currently, there is a community being developed along the Areneuse called "Danson's Grant," named for the original land holder of over 300 years ago.

## Early Churches

Near Portohonk Creek is the **Shiloh Baptist Church** representing the oldest, continuous Baptist congregation in North Carolina, organized in 1727 according to local tradition. In the early 1800's just south of the "Meeting House Bridge" on Portohonk Creek, a shipbuilding facility was built (Forehand, 1977). In fact, local shipyards had been built at several of the creeks along the Pasquotank. During the Civil War, the locally called Battle of Shiloh took place near here. The **Philadelphia Baptist Church** is reported to be the oldest Black congregation established in Camden County. A parishioner told us that the original church was built between 1890 and 1895 as the Philadelphus Baptist Church. About 1940 the school next to the original church burned and sparks from the school caught the church on fire. A new brick structure was built and stands near the site of the original. The church is on Wickham Road, and it is supposed that the road and the original place name came from the English home town of John Archdale who was granted a patent for land here in the late 1600's. Archdale was appointed governor of North (and South) Carolina in 1694 (Pugh, 1953).

# Raymond Creek

This small creek is interesting because it packs a lot of different scenery into a relatively short distance. On a clear calm day, the reflections from the trees on the water might be a reason to call this "Mirror Creek." It's a beautiful waterway with diverse plant and animal life and will make the paddler wish it was a bit longer. One of its unique features is its inland "lake," which may have once been a millpond.

## Location

One of the most southern of the creeks on the east side of the large Pasquotank River, Raymond Creek is south of the community of Shiloh in Camden County.

## Access Point

**A.  SR 1104/Wharf Road**

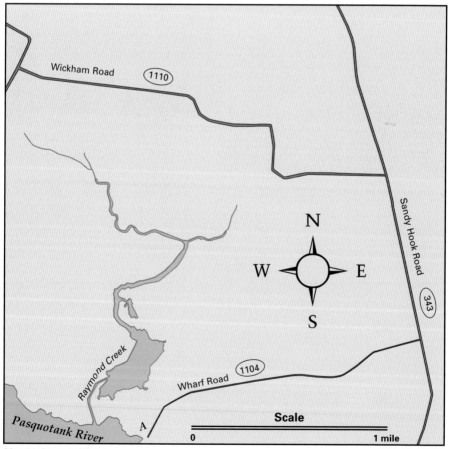

**Map 33:** Raymond Creek

© Vickie Shufer

## Access Point/Paddling Section

### (A) SR 1104/Wharf Road to inland area along Raymond Creek – 2 miles, one way. Camden County, NC

Raymond Creek is hard to spot by road because it has largely been filled in and ditched. From SR 1104/Wickham Road between the communities of Philadelphia, North Carolina and Alder Branch, what is left of this small creek is crossed twice. It is not paddleable unless approached from the Pasquotank at Wharf Bay.

*Directions:* From U.S. 158, almost 1½ miles east of Elizabeth City, take Route 343 south toward Shiloh and continue south to Old Trap. Go west on SR 1104/Wharf Road and follow it to the end. There is a house on each side of the road at the end of SR 1104, but room to park at the turn-around.

The access site is informal, but doable. Please avoid private property. One might have to be creative to keep dry feet. We recommend high boots due to the soft ground at the water's edge and the initial peaty bottom.

Put-in for Raymond Creek                                                    *vs*

### "Old Trap"

Raymond Creek is in the area known as "Old Trap," one of the oldest and first settled areas in Camden County. Old Trap supposedly got its name from a grog shop (tavern) located along the road frequented by sailing men and fishermen on their trips home. Rum imported from the West Indies to the riverside wharves was probably the drink of choice. It is said that the local men's wives called it the "Trap" and later the area became known as "Old Trap" (Pugh, 1953).

Wharf Bay is not very deep, only a foot or two of water for the entire distance to Raymond Creek. Remains of a very long pier into the Pasquotank are visible to the south of the access site indicating the distance to deep water. Perhaps this pier is the remainder of the old wharf that gave this small bay its name. If the water is too shallow due to wind tides, it will be impossible to paddle here. Otherwise, head northwest along the shoreline until a house comes into view. This beautiful log home with an upper deck and a stone chimney is the landmark for Raymond Creek. The small channel that begins Raymond Creek is less than ⅓ of a mile from the put-in.

Log home marking entrance into Raymond Creek                                    *lg*

## *Early Beginnings*

Before 1700 the English settlers of the area set up homesteads on most of the southern creeks of the Pasquotank. At Raymond Creek's joining with the Pasquotank was a commercial landing that supported a small series of buildings and businesses. During the colonial period, ships directly from the West Indies would unload their products here as this was a port of inspection for products being imported or exported (Pugh, 1953). In the September 24, 1806 Norfolk newspaper, *Gazette and Public Ledger,* is an advertisement as follows: "In Camden County at Raymond's Creek on Pasquotank River Shore, a piece of land at a very publick land-ing, where much business has been done to advantage for a number of years, in the heart of the lumber and grain country, containing fourteen acres, on it a good Dwelling-house, with four rooms and plazza. Out houses. A good store, and warehouse separate, both two story" (Pugh and Williams, 1964). There was a shipbuilding business established on Raymond's Creek at "Sloop Landing" circa 1830 (Forehand, 1977).

## River Highlights

After pushing off, and paddling a short distance, the paddler will notice the bottom now is all sand and the water a clear golden color, the result of organic materials containing tannins combining with the water of the Pasquotank. It is possible to observe logs, underwater grasses, clams or whatever is on the bottom of the shallow water.

After passing the log home, the channel, also called "Jimmy's Ditch" by the locals, opens into what appears to be a lake. Surrounding this larger body of water is marshland backed by cypress and pines. The "lake" is about $\frac{4}{10}$ of a mile long and at its northern end a channel off to the east is an alternate route around a marsh island. Shortly after this where the creek is more shaded, wood ducks are likely to be seen, depending on the season.

Beaver work      lg

Continuing from the point where the two channels intersect and heading north, the creek splits left and right, or west and east and is now treed on both sides. Taking the western route first, a lot of small birds frequent the trees and shrubs near the water, pileated woodpeckers may be heard nearby, and turkey vultures and a perhaps a hawk may be seen high overhead. The paddler may begin to see some floating tree branches and pieces of wood chewed by beavers.

Old Man's Beard/SpanishMoss      lg

An hour into the total paddling trip, a beaver dam may block the water trail, depending on water level. Notable along this western route is a lot of oddly shaped cypress knees, resurrection fern, and the unusual old man's beard (see page 111 for a description). Spanish moss is abundant and there are canopied areas that look mysterious and inviting.

The reverse trip to the eastern route is no less interesting and the mosses seem different when backlit by the sun. It is on this return trip that we shared the creek with a curious otter that peered at us, then quickly disappeared.

On the eastern route where the river splits, we were disappointed that deadfall blocked our way only after about 5 minutes of paddling. Returning to the main channel, then back to the put-in site, we wished for a longer trip, but thoroughly enjoyed this beautiful blackwater creek and all it had to offer.

Raymond Creek                                                                      *lg*

## History

Raymond Creek, which has had its name for about 300 years, was previously called Fleming's Creek. One of the first settlers on the northeast side of the Pasquotank River, George Fleming, 1635-1694, never received a title to his land. There is the possibility that he may have purchased the land from the local Indians as was the custom before the land came under the legal ownership of the Lords Proprietors who received this territory from King Charles II in 1663. The other custom was simply to move in, clear some land, and proclaim it as one's own by right of possession. The written information pertaining to George Fleming comes by way of a description in a trial locating "flemins creek" as a boundary line and his will that listed his possessions. The creek changed names to become Raymond Creek within ten years of George Fleming's death (Pugh, 1957). After 1694, the land was patented to William Raymond who died in 1713 leaving 450 acres to his wife, two sons and four daughters (Stevens, 1999). Today, a housing community is being built with the name, "Raymond Creek."

# Newbegun Creek

This small creek is as much fun to get to as it is to paddle. Driving about six miles south of Elizabeth City, North Carolina, one enjoys country views until all of a sudden as if sprouting out of a farm field is a monster of a metal building towering over the pines in the distance. This is an amazing sight from the road and beckons investigation. Driving toward the apparition along the old road between the fields, the trip is cut short by a "No Trespassing" sign. Still it is possible to get close enough to see the aging hangar designed for wartime dirigibles. Tall Stonehenge-like structures are standing nearby. Today the former Naval Station is home to a private industry that is involved in lighter-than-air craft. Back on NC Route 34, the boat ramp for Newbegun Creek is not far.

## Location

Newbegun Creek is the more northern of the two creeks with wide mouths that open into the mighty Pasquotank River south of Elizabeth City. The creek begins as a tiny stream and opens to a half-mile width at Pool Point where it merges with the Intracoastal Waterway, the Pasquotank. With easy access in the village of Weeksville, it is appreciated as a fishing spot.

## Access Point

A. **SR 1132/ Florida Road**
B. **Route 34/ Weeksville Road**

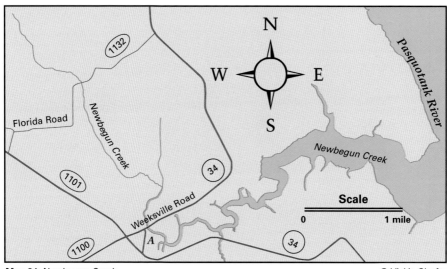

**Map 34:** Newbegun Creek

© Vickie Shufer

## Access Points
### (A) SR 1132/Florida Road

*Directions:* From U.S. 17 (either the Bypass or Business Route) west out of Elizabeth City, take Route 34 south for six miles south to Weeksville. Drive less than ¹⁄₁₀ of a mile south of Sawmill Park on SR 1100/Nixonton Road and turn west on SR 1101/Peartree Road. Look for SR 1132/Florida Road to the north. Olivett's Convenience Store is a landmark here and is a good place to stop for snacks or gasoline. In about 1⁴⁄₁₀ of a mile on Florida Road, be alert for a parking place near the small creek. Park on the southwest or northwest side of the culvert and carry the canoe or kayak across the road to launch. At low water this put-in may be unusable.

Florida Road got its name from that fact that the soil nearby is so sandy and that crops seem to "come up earlier" (Campbell, 2001).

### (B) Route 34/Weeksville Road at Sawmill Park

*Directions:* The Sawmill Park boat ramp is at the intersection of Route 34/ Weeksville Road and SR 1100/Nixonton Road. Route 34 makes a sharp turn to the east here. The boat ramp is on the southeast side of the creek. This site is perfect for launching small boats. There is plenty of parking and a dock for fishing at this fairly new community facility. The park has two picnic tables and trash receptacles and is open from dawn to dusk.

Boat ramp at Sawmill Park                                                            *vs*

## *The World's Largest Wooden Building*

Just south of Elizabeth City, the small community of Weeksville near the Pasquotank River was chosen by the U.S. Government in July of 1941 as the perfect spot to house the great airships or dirigibles called "blimps." The site was close to Norfolk Naval Air Station and conveniently about halfway down the east coast. Since helicopters weren't available yet, these blimps could provide visual inspection of the coastline by looking for foreign submarines during World War II. By August of 1941 the Weeksville Naval Air Station was under construction, eventually providing a home for 850 servicemen, a steel hangar, storage for helium, a mobile mooring mast, landing mat and its own power plant. Known as Dock Number One, it is within easy view from many points from the river.

The following year a second hangar was built of wood and gained fame (until it burned on August 3, 1995) as the world's largest wooden building. In it at the time it burned was the world's largest airship, the *Sentinel 1000.* Neither could be saved and neither was rebuilt.

During World War II, while the blimps were in service, they were lookouts for enemy ships, escorted U.S. ships and participated in search-and-rescue missions. German U-boats were patrolling the coast of Carolina and Virginia and targeting whatever they could. Merchant ships carrying wartime supplies were often hit off the coast of Carolina, already known as the "Graveyard of the Atlantic." The Outer Banks of North Carolina became known as "Torpedo Junction" (Pendergraft, 2001). However, this tragic distinction was soon to change. With the lighter-than-air craft on the lookout, the number of coastal ship casualties fell from one every other day to one about every seventy-five days, proving the value and effectiveness of these eyes in the sky (Mozingo, 2000).

## Paddling Sections

1. (A) SR 1132/Florida Road to (B) Route 34/Weeksville Road – 2 miles, one way.

2. (B) Route 34/Weeksville Road to Pasquotank River – 3 ⁸⁄₁₀ miles, one way.

## Section 1. (A) SR 1132 /Florida Road to (B) Route 34/Weeksville Road – 2 miles, one way. Pasquotank County,

The access site on SR 1132/ Florida Road is on the east side of the double culverts. The water is shallow and the creek can be impassable at low water. It's a short drive from Sawmill Park and easy to inspect. If it looks low at the culvert, drive back to Route 34 and put in at the park's boat ramp. If the way is passable, the paddler will find a very small creek, shady and heavily vegetated. Be alert for the many songbirds that are here. The water is very dark and the water trail inviting.

## Section 2. (B) Route 34/Weeksville Road to Pasquotank River – 3 ⁸⁄₁₀ miles, one way. Pasquotank County

The creek is about 25 feet wide, tree-lined with cypress and water tupelo. A bit of Spanish moss is visible in several trees at the launch site and along the paddling route. The understory near the water is waxmyrtle, black willow and a myriad of vines and wildflowers. The entire creek's length from the ramp to the Pasquotank is three miles. The blackwater creek slowly twists and turns then widens to about a half a mile before entering the Pasquotank River. There are several homes with dredged canals along Newbegun Creek but they do not detract from this blackwater trip.

Newbegun Creek                                                                                          vs

# History Surrounding Newbegun Creek

Across the street to the west of Sawmill Park are two older buildings, circa 1908. The building with the two-tier porch was originally **Turner's Store** and the building beside the river is the old **Weeksville Ginning Company**. These and other late nineteenth and early twentieth century frame structures are clustered in Weeksville, mute testimony of its history as a rural trading and manufacturing center. The **Knox-Davis-Sherlock House** on SR 1100/Nixonton Road is one of the oldest houses in Weeksville, built in the 1820's with double-shouldered chimneys and a front porch similar to the country store in that it also has two tiers. The house has a side entry popular in this area at the time. Another side entry house is the **Sawyer House** on Route 34. The house was built circa 1892 for John H. Sawyer, a prominent local merchant (Bisher and Southern, 1996). A bit south on SR 1100 is the **Newbegun Methodist Church** built circa 1827. During the 1920's the old double entrances on the front were changed to a single entry on the side. The day we visited, we met two very nice women who allowed us to tour the church and the graveyard out back.

The earliest settlements along Newbegun Creek included land grants in the hundreds of acres. These include "Henry Palin, 450 acs. at the mouth of New begin Cr., 25 Sept. 1653" (Nugent, 1992). Apparently Mr. Palin, if he set up a homestead here, had no neighbors until ten years later when three men were granted land: Robert Lawry, William Jennings, and Phillip Evans. To read one of their grants, "Robert Lawry, 300 acs. in a bay at the mouth of New begin Creek, beg. at the mouth of a small swamp which parts this & land of Henry Palin, running S.W. &c. up the said Cr. To a marked gum in the midst of the mouth of a great swamp which parts this & land of Mr. Jennings &c. 25 Sept. 1663" (Nugent, 1992), one wonders about the unnamed surveyor who explored the uninhabited swamps and creeks off the Pasquotank River or the settler who cleared the land, built a home and planted crops.

As home sites along Newbegun Creek were built and settlements along all of the local Carolina waterways were established, the rivers served as highways until roadways were built in the 1700's. The early legislative bodies and judicial courts were held in private homes and Newbegun Creek was the site of the "court house" for Pasquotank Precinct for many years. In 1727 the first real courthouse was erected on an acre of land purchased from Thomas Palin, possibly a relative of our first landowner on Newbegun Creek, Henry Palin.

## The Naming of Carolina and the Forming of Several Tidewater Counties

In 1663, King Charles II of England repaid the eight noblemen who had helped him regain the throne (in 1660) of Charles I, his father. These eight men became known as the Lords Proprietors and they were given a large tract of land bordered by the Atlantic Ocean to the east, the colony of Virginia to the north, and part of the area of present-day Florida to the south. The area was named "Carolina" from the Latin word for "Charles," carolus. The first governor was appointed in 1664 and with a government beginning, the County of Albemarle and the Albemarle Sound were named for one of the Proprietors, George Monck, the Duke of Albemarle. In 1670, as more areas became settled, the County of Albemarle was split into the four precincts of Chowan, Currituck, Pasquotank, and Perquimans. In 1739 Currituck and Pasquotank Counties were formed, and in 1777, Camden County.

## A Timeline of Events Related to the Colonies of Virginia and North Carolina

1584    Queen Elizabeth gives patent to Sir Walter Raleigh to establish a colony in the New World

1585    Colony of Roanoke with 100 people is founded

1585    After 10 months Roanoke colonists board ships of Sir Francis Drake and return to England, 15 of Drake's men stay, never to be seen again

1587    Roanoke's second colony founded with 116 people

1590    Remembered as "The Lost Colony," the second colony vanishes leaving the word "Croatan" carved on a tree

1602    Sir Walter Raleigh hires Samuel Mace to search for 1587 colonists

1603    Death of Queen Elizabeth. James is crowned king.

1606    James I, issues charter for the Virginia Company of London to establish colony in New World

1607    First permanent English colony settles at Jamestown, Virginia

1608    John Smith attempts to send men in search of the 1587 colonists to the Chowan region

| | |
|---|---|
| 1625 | Death of James I. Charles I ascends throne |
| 1627 | Barbados in the West Indies becomes an English Colony |
| 1638 | County of Norfolk formed, includes territory to 35 degrees north latitude, about where Ocracoke Inlet is today |
| 1646 | Expedition from Virginia to deal with "Indian Problem" led by Richard Bennett (by land) and by Thomas Dew (by water) |
| 1649 | Death of Charles I (beheaded) in England |
| 1654 | Francis Yeardley and a group of six others visited Currituck Sound area |
| 1660 | Charles II restored to the British throne |
| 1663 | Eight Lords Proprietors named by Charles II granted all of Carolina (the first use of the name, Carolina) |
| 1665 | Charles II extends boundary of Carolina |
| 1670 | Albemarle County is split into Precincts of Chowan, Currituck, Pasquotank, and Perquimans |
| 1677 | Culpeper's Rebellion against acting Governor Miller near present-day Elizabeth City |
| 1685 | Death of Charles II, James II ascends throne |
| 1688 | James II deposed |
| 1689 | William and Mary ascend English throne |
| 1691 | Beginning of the division of Carolina into two parts by the establishment of a deputy governor in the Albemarle region |
| 1712 | First Governor of NC, Edward Hyde of Edenton, appointed by Lords Proprietors |
| 1728 | Survey of boundary line between Virginia and North Carolina by team of representatives of both colonies, VA and NC |
| 1729 | Surrender of Lords Proprietors' charter; NC under direct authority of British Crown |
| 1739 | Currituck and Pasquotank Counties formed |
| 1763 | Earliest known survey map of the lake now known as Lake Drummond in Virginia prepared by Gershom Nimmo for George Washington |

# Big Flatty Creek

Big Flatty Creek is a beauty. Virtually deserted except for an occassional fisherman, this cypress-lined creek has a true wilderness feel. The creek is about half a mile wide at the launch site and widens slowly to the confluence with Albemarle Sound to the south. Few houses are visible from the creek.

Of the five feeder creeks to Big Flatty, two are noteworthy. Mill Dam and Chapel Creek can be accessed by paddling west across the Big Flatty to the opposite shoreline. Continue west and north until a V-shaped fork is seen. Mill Dam Creek is the first tributary to the west, followed by Chapel Creek.

## Location

Big Flatty is located about 14 miles southeast of Elizabeth City by water. It is the most southern of Pasquotank County's creeks and flows into the Albemarle Sound.

## Access Point

A.  **NC Wildlife Resources Commission Boat Ramp - SR 1108/ Shadneck Road**

B.  **SR 1103/Esclip Road, via Mill Dam Creek and Chapel Creek**

Boat launch at the NC Wildlife Resources Commission Boat Ramp                    *vs*

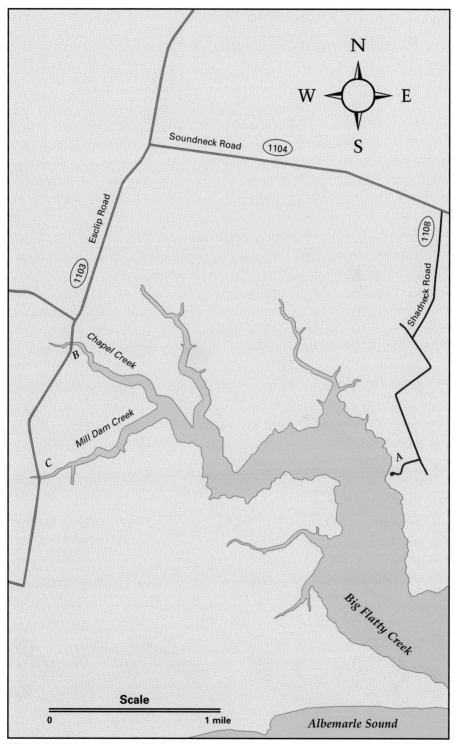

N
W E
S

Soundneck Road (1104)

Esclip Road

(1103)

(1108)

Shadneck Road

Chapel Creek

B

Mill Dam Creek

C

A

Big Flatty Creek

Scale

0                    1 mile

Albemarle Sound

**Map 35:** Big Flatty to Mill Dam Creek and Chapel Creek                    © Vickie Shufer

# Access Points/Paddling Section
## (A) SR 1108/Shadneck Road

*Directions*: From U.S. 17 in Elizabeth City, follow Route 34 south to Weeksville and turn south on SR 1103/Esclip Road. Continue about one mile to the intersection of SR 1104/Soundneck Road and turn east. Follow this country road for about 2 miles to the intersection of SR 1108/Shadneck Road and turn south. After 2 miles, the paved road ends. The road to the boat ramp is a turn to the west and is marked with a North Carolina Wildlife Resources Commission Access sign.

There are no activities allowed here except for boat launching and parking. There are no facilities, picnic tables or trash receptacles. The paddler will want to remember to bring along a spare trash bag to leave the area cleaner than it was found. Tall trees border the large parking area and it is possible to find a shaded parking spot. There is ample room for many vehicles. The concrete boat ramp is at the western end of the access area.

Depending on wind direction, this waterway could be a challenge for a canoe or kayak trip as the creek is wide and the water can be very choppy. On a calm day, or with wind from the east or northeast, head west and there is much to explore. Two miles to the northwest are Chapel Creek and Mill Dam Creek, two tributaries that fork to the west of the larger Big Flatty Creek. For access from these creeks, see page 219.

To the south, the paddle trip to the Pasquotank River is 2 miles. The river widens considerably and we suggest caution if paddling a canoe or kayak as the wind can make the water quite rough.

## River Highlights

There are several coves and tributaries to explore on a calm day. After taking a break in one cove on the south bank, we noticed beyond the trees a grazing field for cows and/or horses, adding to the rural feeling of the area. The water has provided fish as a staple since colonial times.

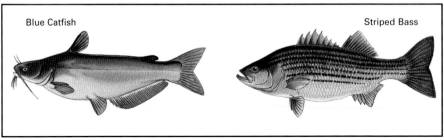

Blue Catfish    Striped Bass

*Illustrations by Carl "Spike" Knuth*

# Chapel Creek/Mill Dam Creek

The V-shaped route of these tributaries of Big Flatty Creek have the look of two other creeks, one with a familiar name: Areneuse and Mill Dam Creek in Camden County. These four water trails only look alike on a map. The resemblance ends there as the paddler will discover and the authors will describe in the next two pages.

Just south of the first creek is the Union United Methodist Church, founded in 1826, and perhaps the origin of Chapel Creek's name.

## Location

Chapel Creek and Mill Dam Creek are tributaries of Big Flatty Creek that empty into the Albemarle Sound about 14 miles southeast of Elizabeth City by water.

## Access Point

A. SR 1103/Esclip Road - Mill Dam Creek or Chapel Creek

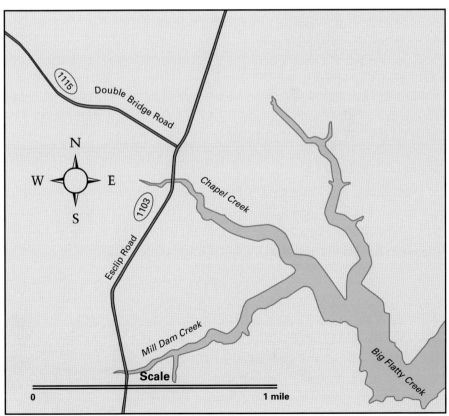

**Map 36:** Mill Dam Creek and Chapel Creek

© Vickie Shufer

## Access Point/Paddling Section

# A. SR 1103/Esclip Road - Mill Dam Creek to Chapel Creek, Pasquotank County – 1¾ miles, one way

Located in an agricultural community with few homesites, these creeks can be paddled in a single trip without running a shuttle. The access sites for both creeks are less than a mile apart on SR 1103/Esclip Road, so it is possible to walk back to the put-in site to pick up the car used in the drive to the first site, similar to Areneuse and Mill Dam Creeks of Camden County. There is very little traffic on this back road and the trip on the twin creeks is quiet except for bird or insect sounds, dissimilar to Areneuse and the other Mill Dam Creek.

We suggest beginning on Chapel Creek, go upstream first, then paddle into the big waters of Big Flatty, Go southwest to complete the trip by paddling upstream on Mill Dam Creek. Mill Dam Creek is smaller than Chapel. The double culverts of Mill Dam Creek are too small to paddle through so if the paddler wants to paddle further upstream, a portage is required.

*Directions:* To get to the twin creeks from Elizabeth City, drive south on NC Route 34 to SR 1103/Esclip Road, about 3 miles southeast of Weeksville, NC. Follow SR 1103/Esclip Road south to the crossing of Chapel Creek, just south of SR 1115/Double Bridge Road. Drive to the next creek to the south and check the water level to see if it is possible to put in at Mill Dam. If it does not look like a put-in is possible, just drive back to Chapel Creek and park on either side of the bridge. The easiest access is on the southeast side of the bridge. Deadfall may hamper this trip, so it may be wise to bring a saw or pruners.

## River Highlights

Both Chapel and Mill Dam Creek are small and mossy, wild and inviting. Chapel Creek is the larger of the two small creeks, about forty feet wide and bordered by young trees. The water is deeper and easier to paddle than on Mill Dam. A bit of current may be discerned, depending on time of year and recent rainfall which slowly drains from the upper stretches of Chapel Creek.

In this farm community we were surprised to see that so much wildlife was along the banks of the creek as well as in the creek. There were several people bank-fishing at Esclip Road's crossing of Mill Dam Creek on a recent visit. They reported that they had fished there for years. When the fishermen were asked what types of fish were caught besides the catfish that we saw, they said, "The good eatin' kind."

Channel Catfish

*Illustration by Carl "Spike" Knuth*

222

Spanish moss is everywhere. In the spring, look for the small yellow-green flower with three petals. For something so small, it has a lot of fragrance.

The real thrill came when we spotted the dwarf palmetto, a close relative of the cabbage palm. It is most commonly seen in Florida, Georgia and South Carolina. Even though it is cold-hardy, it requires hot summers to survive. The large, fan-shaped leaves stand out in the understory of the forest. An interesting feature is that the trunk is underground, making it appear more shrub-like rather than tree-like. Small white flowers appear in early summer followed by the fruit which is a small drupe

*vs*

that turns dark blue in the fall. The fruits provide food for robins, fish crows and raccoons. This palmetto discovery is a natural treasure.

Dwarf palmettoes along the banks of Chapel Creek                    *lg*

Part Seven


*Little River*

*and its tributaries*

# Little River

The Little River is fairly true to its name, at least in the headwaters. Although it is narrower than its neighbors which run parallel to it (North River, Pasquotank River to the east and the Perquimans and Chowan to the west), it is still 1 to 1½ miles across from Truebloods Point near Nixonton, and at its confluence with the Albemarle Sound at Stevenson Point, the Little River is two miles across.

Unfortunately, the headwaters of the creek are unpaddleable due to the very narrow size and the deadfall which blocks the paddler's path. We have not been able to paddle very far north of the Old U.S. 17 access site, although the upper swamp looks cool and inviting.

The Little River can be accessed from Old U.S. 17 near the community of Rabbit Corner and the Little River's two Pasquotank County tributaries,

## Location

Little River is midway between the cities of Elizabeth City in Pasquotank County and Hertford in Perquimans County and is the dividing line between these two counties for its entire length. The path of the Little River begins in the farmland in the southern part of the Great Dismal Swamp near the community of Parkville. It travels basically northwest to southeast through swampy land crossed by only four roads for its entire 17 mile path until it joins Albemarle Sound.

## Access Point
A. Old U.S. 17

Little River with Halls Creek on left

lg

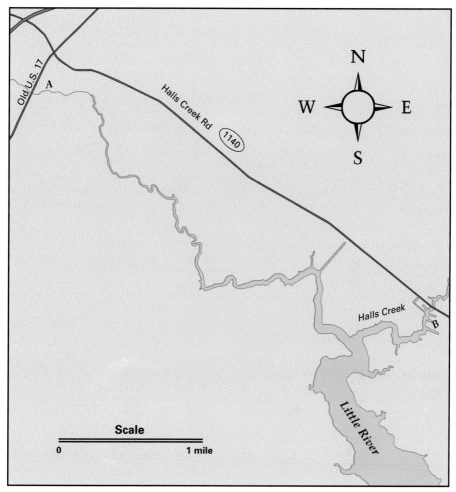

**Map 37:** Little River to Halls Creek

© Vickie Shufer

Symonds Creek and Halls Creek. These two tributaries offer boaters an opportunity to experience the quiet water of the smaller creeks and the long view and larger, wider water of Little River.

## Access Point/Paddling Section

### (A) Old U.S. 17 to SR 1140/Halls Creek Road - 4.6 miles, one way. Pasquotank County, NC

*Directions*: From Elizabeth City, take U.S. 17 By-pass south approximately 4 miles to the intersection of Old U.S. 17 and turn southeast (left). After a couple of miles, cross Halls Creek Road/SR 1140, and continue on Old U.S. 17 until just before the bridge at Rabbit Corner. On the southeast side of Old

Little River launch site from Old U.S. 17                                    *vs*

U.S. 17, there is a boat ramp and public parking area large enough to accommodate 10 vehicles with trailers.

Boats can be launched from the small, wooden dock at the southeast end of the parking/turn-around area. Be careful not to step out too far into the water as it abruptly becomes deeper, about 4' deep off the end of the dock. This access point is listed in the *North Carolina Coastal Plain Paddle Trails Guide*. Contact the Albemarle Resource Conservation and Development Council, 730 Granville Street, Edenton, NC, 27932 for additonal information.

## *River Highlights*

This easy and comfortable paddle route begins in the narrow part of the Little River where it truly lives up to its name. Overhung with many trees, the first part of the route is shady during the summer months. There is a bit of current flowing south, making the paddling a bit easier than some other local streams. Depending on water level, the current will vary from not noticeable to helpful. At certain times of the year, duckweed may be found floating on the surface (see page 95).

The number of wood duck nesting boxes seen on this trail suggests a healthy population of wood ducks, and indeed, they were the first wildlife we saw. Wood ducks naturally nest in cavities of dead or dying trees. They leave the nest soon after hatching and stay close to their mother while traveling through the swamp.

There are a few privately owned cabins that can be seen along the way. A derelict cabin is seen first and the second cabin, currently in use, is near mile marker 2 of the **Albemarle Regional Canoe Trail System**. Look for the white marker on the west side (river left) of the creek. It is near this locale that we spotted

Wood duck box                                                    lg

some beaver work in the woods. In a few seconds, we spotted a small beaver swimming close to shore.

Fishing cabin on Little River               vs

Just a few more houses are scattered along the route, less than six total, as of this publication date. One would hope that the area develops slowly if at all, due to the many animal and plant species that can be seen along the water's edge.

As the Little River winds through hardwood swamps, it grows steadily wider, becoming about fifty yards wide at the entrance to Halls Creek. At this point Halls Creek is about the same size as Little River and the junction is marked by canoe trail mile marker 4 to the southeast and is easy to spot.

To paddle to Halls Creek access site, travel northeast on Halls Creek about a half-mile to the **North Carolina Wildlife Resources Commission Boat Ramp** on SR 1140/Halls Creek Road. Look for the trailer park and brown access sign. The turn for the take-out is to the south (right) between the red and green posts in the water. Driving directions are in the Halls Creek section.

Just after the confluence with Halls Creek the Little River is suddenly ⅓ of a mile across. It just gets wider until reaching the Albemarle Sound at the tip of Pasquotank County across to Stevenson Point in Perquimans County, a width of a little over 2 miles. There are no public access spots along this larger part of the Little River.

# Halls Creek

This historic little creek is part of the *North Carolina Coastal Plain Paddle Trails Guide*. A blackwater creek, like its neighbors, the Little River and Symonds Creek, it gets its color from tannins produced by the various trees along the creek.

## Access Point

### (A) SR 1140/Halls Creek Road to Little River – ⁹⁄₁₀ mile. Pasquotank County

*Directions*: From Elizabeth City, take U.S. 17 By-pass south approximately 4 miles to the intersection of Old U.S. 17 and turn southeast (left). Go about 2 miles until you come to SR

## Location

Halls Creek, a Pasquotank County tributary of the Little River, is located on SR 1140/Halls Creek Road about 6 miles southwest of Elizabeth City. The creek begins in swampland to the north near SR 1144/Simpson Ditch Road and becomes wider and paddleable near the boat ramp on Halls Creek Road.

## Access Point

A. SR 1140/Halls Creek Road

Little River with Halls Creek on left                                      *lg*

1140/Halls Creek Road, and go east (left) approximately 2½ miles. Look for the North Carolina Wildlife Resources Commission Boat Ramp sign. This is the access for canoes, kayaks, and small boats. The turn for the access is to the south (right) between the red and green posts in the water. The gravel parking area is a loop road that can be accessed from the east or west on Halls Creek Road with ample space for many vehicles and trailers. The single ramp is paved and is bordered by a small wooden pier.

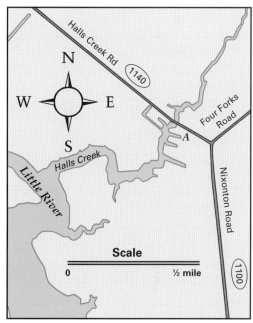

**Map 38:** Halls Creek to Little River        © Vickie Shufer

Boat ramp at Halls Creek        *vs*

## Paddling Sections

1. **(A) SR 1140/Halls Creek Road to headwaters – mileage variable. Pasquotank County, NC**

2. **(A) SR 1140/Halls Creek Road to Little River – %10 mile, one way, or total mileage variable by continuing south. Pasquotank County, NC**

## Section 1. (A) SR 1140/ Halls Creek Road to head-waters – mileage variable. Pasquotank County, NC

Halls Creek begins in swampland near SR 1144/Simpson Ditch Road. At this point it is little more than a ditch. Fallen trees and debris prevent paddling from this site. If you want to explore the headwaters, put-in at the boat ramp on Halls Creek Road and head north. A portage is required over Halls Creek Road after departing from the launch site. The current bridge is lower than the former bridge and can rarely be paddled under, even by a solo kayaker at low water levels. Use caution when crossing the road as there are fast moving vehicles, even though this is not a major road. After relaunching, the paddler will see no houses on this part of Halls Creek. Although the trip is short, the creek is beautiful. See how far you can paddle on this upper stretch. Sometimes the greatest rewards come form a little more effort.

## Section 2. (A) SR 1140/Halls Creek Road to Little River – %10 mile, one way, or total mileage variable by continuing south. Pasquotank County, NC

Departing by boat from the launch area, the paddler will notice the small pasture lands along the banks and perhaps the Canada geese which have recently claimed it. Great blue herons, green-backed herons, and belted kingfishers watch from their perches as paddlers leave the civilized part of the creek for the natural area beckoning to the west. The creek becomes increasingly wider as it approaches Little River. At its widest it is still quite a small creek. It retains its size until the confluence with the Little River, at which point both appear to be the same size. To the paddler, it may appear that Halls Creek makes a right turn to the north, but this is the Little River's northern path.

Green-backed heron                    lg

232

# History

In 1664, William Drummond was appointed as the first governor for Albemarle County. That same year three counties were to be established in Carolina: Albemarle, Clarendon (Cape Fear River area), and Craven which was later to be South Carolina. The first Albemarle Assembly met near the banks of Halls Creek as early as 1665. There may have been a particular building erected for the purposes of the Assembly meetings, but more likely, these meetings were held at someone's home. According to local tradition, this first meeting took place under a large oak tree near the creek.

Almost all early travel involving any distance was accomplished by boat as the few roadways were ill-kept and not much more than trails. Waterways were the first highways and the fact that such an important meeting took place at Halls Creek may have meant that it was a protected waterway, centrally located or in the vicinity of the homes of the early legislators in the colony.

In honor of the first Albemarle Assembly, a commemorative stone has been placed opposite the entrance to the boat ramp parking area on SR 1140/Halls Creek Road. Look for the two-story Ruritan Club Meeting House and the stone will be just to the east of the driveway.

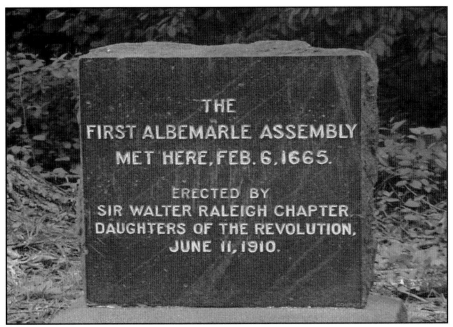

*lg*

# Symonds Creek

Symonds Creek is sheltered and attractive as a paddling stream. It begins narrow and shady but after leaving the bridge on SR 1100/Nixonton Road, it quickly widens. Like many of the streams in this part of North Carolina, Symonds Creek is not very long, but can be extended by paddling east on Matthews Creek, about ¼ mile south of the bridge. It can also be combined with other creeks in the area, making it possible to enjoy paddling several coastal waterways in a day.

## Location

Symonds Creek is a tributary of Little River which empties into the Albemarle Sound about 17 miles southeast of Elizabeth City by water.

## Access Point

A. SR 1100/Nixonton Road - Boat Ramp

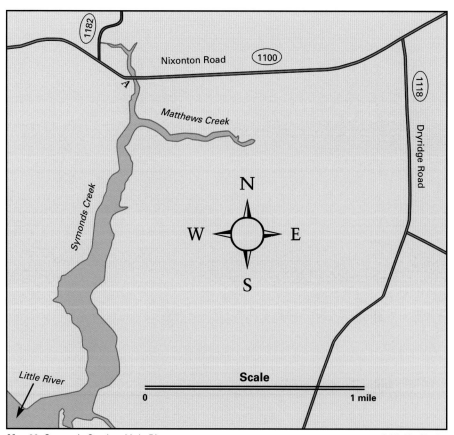

**Map 39:** Symonds Creek to Little River

© Vickie Shufer

# Access Point
## *(A) SR 1100/Nixonton Road - Boat Ramp*

*Directions:* From Elizabeth City, take U.S. 17 south to the intersection of Old U.S. 17 and go east/southeast (left). Follow this to SR 1140/Halls Creek Road and turn east (left). Go almost 3¼ miles to the intersection of Nixonton Road and go south. After 1¼ miles, Nixonton Road makes a sharp turn to the east and becomes SR 1100. Continue for another 2⁵⁄₁₀ miles until you come to a small bridge. The parking area is just before the bridge on the southwest side of the creek. Please note that on some maps, SR 1100 is referred to as Symonds Creek Road and on the current road signs, the road is named Nixonton Road.

This access point is listed in the *North Carolina Coastal Plain Paddle Trails Guide*. This rather informal site can hold quite a few cars, but be careful not to encroach upon private land that is adjacent and marked. Fishing line can be seen tangled in the overhead lines at the side of the bridge, offering mute testimony of the favorite activity here. Small motor boats are occasionally seen, but this area seems fairly undiscovered by paddlers.

Boat ramp at Nixonton Road    *vs*

## Paddling Sections

1. (A) SR 1100/Nixonton Road Boat Ramp to SR 1182/ Meads Town Road, ¼ mile, Pasquotank County, NC

2. (A) SR 1100/Nixonton Road Boat Ramp to Little River – 2 miles. Pasquotank County, NC

## Section 1. (A) SR 1100/ Nixonton Road Boat Ramp to SR 1182/Meads Town Road – ¼ mile, Pasquotank County, NC

If the water level is low enough to allow passage under the bridge, it is well worth the effort. The upper part of Symonds Creek is narrow and shady and has a lot to be seen, even though it only goes ¼ mile before coming to SR 1182/Meads Town Road. The creek continues on the other side of the road but fallen trees and other natural debris make paddling impossible. At lower water levels, there is not enough water in the upper creeks to float a canoe or kayak and deadfall is common.

Bordering the creek are swamp blackgum and bald cypress trees with spanish moss draped over their branches. Waxmyrtle, winterberry and even dwarf palmettoes were growing in the understory. We saw wood ducks, hairy woodpeckers, and a kingfisher on this short stretch of waterway.

Winterberry                                                                                    *vs*

## Section 2. (A) SR 1100/Nixonton Road Boat Ramp to Little River – 2 miles. Pasquotank County, NC

The abundance of kingfishers on this water trail also is a good indication that fishing is good here. Other fish-eating birds include great blue herons and cormorants. Small motorboats are occasionally seen, but this area seems fairly undiscovered by paddlers.

The trip to the Little River gives the paddler a view of the long fetch of the Little River and a look at a new community being built on the southwest creek bank near the confluence with the Little River. We nick-named this waterway "The Kingfisher Trail" as so many of these birds were flying across our watery path making a loud rattling call while on the wing. Perhaps the fishing is good for birds as well as people.

Photo by Paul Shufer

Double-crested Cormorant

Cormorants are diving birds that prey on fish while swimming underwater. They lack oil glands in their wings and are frequently seen perched on a log with their wings spread outward to dry. When alarmed, they will often dive underwater rather than taking flight.

Great blue herons are tall, wading birds that can be spotted along the shoreling stalking their prey. They use their long, pointed beaks as a spear to catch fish swimming near. When alarmed, they give a deep, harsh call as they take flight.

There are no public access points to Symonds Creek in this southerly direction unless the paddler continues on the Little River. Big Flatty Creek is a total of about 13 miles south of the confluence which includes a lot of open water. This could be tiring and dangerous on any day and we cannot recommend it. To paddle north to a take-out site would put the paddler at SR1140/Halls Creek Road access, a total of about 7 miles by water. There is still a lot of open water from Long Point to Truebloods Point before the opening to Halls Creek. Neither of the longer trips is recommended for novice paddlers. We can recommend an out-and-back trip. Just keep an eye on the weather and the time.

# History

Both Symonds and Newbegun Creek were settled more safely than larger rivers where moorage and weather conditions made settlement more difficult. Both creeks were settled during the early history of this part of coastal Carolina. As commerce was accomplished along the waterways, inspection stations for the shipment of pork, beef, rice, tar, pitch, turpentine, staves, headings, shingles, and lumber were mandated by the Colonial General Assembly of North Carolina. At least by 1755, Symonds Creek had two such stations. One was listed at "Symon's Bridge" and another at the mouth of "Symon's Creek." Reading further in the *State Records of North Carolina*, one finds the same listings for the year 1758, although the creek that year is spelled "Simon's." By 1770, the records no longer mention Symonds Creek as an inspection port even though a small farming community had developed there. As the colonists discovered, this is indeed a beautiful area in which to live. There is still a community named Symonds Creek and the creek is sheltered and attractive as a paddling stream.

Symonds Creek

*vs*

# Epilogue

To keep this book a reasonable size we had to make several decisions about a couple of waterways that might have been appropriate. Two creeks which originate in the Dismal Swamp were omitted from this book. Shingle Creek in Suffolk, Virginia, that connects to the Nansemond River, is west of our boundary and will be included in a forthcoming book. The Perquimmans River originates in the southern part of the Great Dismal Swamp in North Carolina and empties into the Albemarle Sound. It also will be included in a forthcoming book that will include Merchants Mill Pond and Lassiter Swamp.

As you paddle these waterways, be aware that Hurricane Isabel, in September, 2003, dealt a brutal blow to northeastern North Carolina and southeastern Virginia. Consider organizing a river clean-up crew to help open navigable paths for future paddlers. While we have made all attempts to be correct, change does occur. We hope you will inform us of any changes that you experience while exploring these waterways.

Thank you and happy paddling!

*– Lillie Gilbert and Vickie Shufer*

# Checklists

## Latin names for plants listed in text by common name

| | | |
|---|---|---|
| \_\_\_\_\_ | Arum, Arrow | *Peltandra virginica* |
| \_\_\_\_\_ | Ash | *Fraxinus caroliniana* |
| \_\_\_\_\_ | Asters | *Aster* spp. |
| \_\_\_\_\_ | Azalea, Swamp | *Rhododendron viscosum* |
| \_\_\_\_\_ | Blackberry | *Rubus* spp. |
| \_\_\_\_\_ | Bulltongue | *Sagittaria falcata* |
| \_\_\_\_\_ | Buttonbush | *Cephalanthus occidentalis* |
| \_\_\_\_\_ | Cardinal Flower | *Lobelia cardinalis* |
| \_\_\_\_\_ | Cattails | *Typha latifolia* |
| \_\_\_\_\_ | Cherry, Black | *Prunus serotina* |
| \_\_\_\_\_ | Chokeberry, Red | *Aronia arbutifolia* |
| \_\_\_\_\_ | Climbing Hempweed | *Mikania scandens* |
| \_\_\_\_\_ | Cordgrass, Big | *Spartina cynosuroides* |
| \_\_\_\_\_ | Cypress, Bald | *Taxodium distichum* |
| \_\_\_\_\_ | Cypress, Pond | *Taxodium ascendens* |
| \_\_\_\_\_ | Cyrilla | *Cyrilla racemosa* |
| \_\_\_\_\_ | Dodder | *Cuscuta gronovii* |
| \_\_\_\_\_ | Dogwood, Swamp | *Cornus stricta* |
| \_\_\_\_\_ | Duckweed | *Spirodela polyrhiza* |
| \_\_\_\_\_ | Elderberry | *Sambucus canadensis* |
| \_\_\_\_\_ | Fern, Marsh | *Thelypteris palustris* |
| \_\_\_\_\_ | Fern, Resurrection | *Polypodium polypodioides* |
| \_\_\_\_\_ | Fern, Royal | *Osmunda regalis* |
| \_\_\_\_\_ | Flag, Blue | *Iris virginica* |
| \_\_\_\_\_ | Goldenrod | *Solidago* spp. |
| \_\_\_\_\_ | Grape, Muscadine | *Vitis rotundifolia* |
| \_\_\_\_\_ | Greenbrier, Common | *Smilax rotundifolia* |
| \_\_\_\_\_ | Groundnuts | *Apios americana* |
| \_\_\_\_\_ | Groundsel Bush | *Baccharis halimifolia* |
| \_\_\_\_\_ | Hawthorn | *Crataegus* spp. |
| \_\_\_\_\_ | Jewelweed | *Impatiens capensis* |
| \_\_\_\_\_ | Leather Flower | *Clematis crispa* |
| \_\_\_\_\_ | Lily, Turk's Cap | *Lilium superbum* |
| \_\_\_\_\_ | Lily, Yellow Pond | *Nuphar luteum* |
| \_\_\_\_\_ | Lizard's Tail | *Saururus cernuus* |
| \_\_\_\_\_ | Maleberry | *Lyonia ligustrina* |

| | | |
|---|---|---|
| _____ | Mallow, Rose | *Hibiscus moscheutos* |
| _____ | Maple, Red | *Acer rubrum* |
| _____ | Milkweed, Swamp | *Asclepias incarnata* |
| _____ | Mistletoe | *Phoradendron sertotinum* |
| _____ | Mulberry, Red | *Morus rubra* |
| _____ | Needlerush, Black | *Juncus roemerianus* |
| _____ | Oak, Pin | *Quercus palustris* |
| _____ | Old Man's Beard | *Usnea* spp. |
| _____ | Palmetto, Dwarf | *Sabal minor* |
| _____ | Pawpaw | *Asimina triloba* |
| _____ | Pepperbush, Sweet | *Clethra alnifolia* |
| _____ | Phragmites | *Phragmites australis* |
| _____ | Pickerelweed | *Pontederia cordata* |
| _____ | Pignut Hickory | *Carya glabra* |
| _____ | Pine, Loblolly | *Pinus taeda* |
| _____ | Poison Ivy | *Rhus toxicodendron* |
| _____ | Possum Haw | *Viburnum nudum* |
| _____ | Redbay | *Persea borbonia* |
| _____ | Redcedar, Eastern | *Juniperus virginiana* |
| _____ | Rose, Swamp | *Rosa palustris* |
| _____ | Saltmarsh Cordgrass | *Spartina alterniflora* |
| _____ | Sassafras | *Sassafras albidum* |
| _____ | Sawgrass | *Cladium jamaicense* |
| _____ | Sedge, Epiphytic | *Carex decomposita* |
| _____ | Seedbox, Winged | *Ludwigia alata* |
| _____ | Silky Camelia | *Stewartia malecodendron* |
| _____ | Spanish Moss | *Tillandsia usneoides* |
| _____ | Spatterdock | *Nuphar luteum* |
| _____ | Sundrops | *Oenothera fruticosa* |
| _____ | Swamp Sweetbells | *Leucothoe racemosa* |
| _____ | Sweetbay Magnolia | *Magnolia virginiana* |
| _____ | Sweetflag | *Acorus calamus* |
| _____ | Sweetgum | *Liquidambar styraciflua* |
| _____ | Sycamore | *Platanus occidentalis* |
| _____ | Tupelo, Water | *Nyssa aquatica* |
| _____ | Water Lily, Fragrant | *Nymphaea odorata* |
| _____ | Waxmyrtle | *Myrica cerifera* |
| _____ | Willow, Black | *Salix nigra* |
| _____ | Winterberry | *Ilex decidua* |

# Bird Checklist

## Cormorants
_____ Double-crested Cormorant

## Herons and Egrets
_____ Great Blue Heron
_____ Green-backed Heron
_____ Great Egret

## Vultures
_____ Black Vulture
_____ Turkey Vulture

## Eagle, Osprey, Owls, Hawks
_____ Bald Eagle
_____ Osprey
_____ Barred Owl
_____ Sharp-shinned Hawk
_____ Red-tailed Hawk
_____ Red-shouldered Hawk
_____ Cooper's Hawk
_____ Broad-winged Hawk

## Ducks
_____ Mallard
_____ Black Duck
_____ Wood Duck
_____ Canada Geese
_____ Tundra Swans
_____ Snow Geese

## Gulls and Terns
_____ Herring Gull
_____ Ring-billed Gull
_____ Common Tern

## Sandpipers
_____ Spotted Sandpiper
_____ Common Snipe
_____ American Woodcock

## Kingfisher
_____ Belted Kingfisher

## Blackbirds and Orioles
_____ Red-winged Blackbird
_____ Rusty Blackbird
_____ Common Grackle
_____ Brown-headed Cowbird

## Crows and Jays
_____ Common Crow
_____ Fish Crow
_____ Blue Jay

## Hummingbird
_____ Ruby-throated Hummingbird

## Woodpeckers
_____ Common Flicker
_____ Pileated Woodpecker
_____ Hairy Woodpecker
_____ Downy Woodpecker
_____ Red-bellied Woodpecker
_____ Yellow-bellied Sapsucker

## Warblers
_____ Yellow-rumped Warbler
_____ Black-and-White Warbler
_____ Blue-winged Warbler
_____ Common Yellowthroat
_____ Pine Warbler
_____ Prothonotary Warbler
_____ American Redstart
_____ Ovenbird

## Vireos
_____ White-eyed Vireo
_____ Red-eyed Vireo

## Thrushes, Robins, and Bluebirds
_____ Wood Thrush
_____ Hermit Thrush
_____ American Robin
_____ Gray Catbird

## Flycatchers
_____ Great Crested Flycatcher
_____ Eastern Kingbird
_____ Eastern Phoebe
_____ Eastern Wood Pewee

## Wrens, Gnatcatchers & Kinglets
_____ Marsh Wren
_____ Carolina Wren
_____ Blue-gray Gnatcatcher

## Chickadees and Titmice
_____ Carolina Chickadee
_____ Tufted Titmouse

## Doves
_____ Mourning Dove

## Nuthatches and Creepers
_____ White-breasted Nuthatch
_____ Brown-headed Nuthatch
_____ Brown Creeper

## Swallows
_____ Tree Swallow
_____ Barn Swallow
_____ Purple Martin

## Cuckoos
_____ Yellow-billed Cuckoo

## Waxwings
_____ Cedar Waxwing

## Cardinals and Finches
_____ Northern Cardinal
_____ American Goldfinch
_____ Pine Siskin
_____ Indigo Bunting

## Sparrows and Juncos
_____ Song Sparrow
_____ White-throated Sparrow
_____ Chipping Sparrow
_____ Dark-eyed Junco

# Game and Fur-Bearing Mammals
_____ Beaver
_____ Black Bear
_____ Bobcat
_____ Fox, Gray
_____ Fox, Red
_____ Mink
_____ Muskrat
_____ Nutria
_____ Opossum
_____ Otter, River
_____ Rabbit, Eastern Cottontail
_____ Rabbit, Marsh
_____ Raccoon
_____ Squirrel, Gray
_____ Deer, White-tailed

# Reptiles and Amphibians

**Turtles**
____ Eastern Box Turtle
____ Mud Turtle
____ Painted Turtle
____ Red-bellied Turtle
____ River Cooter
____ Snapping Turtle
____ Spotted Turtle
____ Stinkpot
____ Yellow-bellied Turtle

**Snakes**
____ Brown Water Snake
____ Canebrake Rattlesnake
____ Copperhead
____ Cottonmouth
____ Mud Snake
____ Northern Water Snake
____ Red-bellied Water Snake

**Lizards**
____ Broadhead Skink

____ Fence Lizard
____ Five-lined Skink
____ Glass Lizard

**Salamanders**
____ Marbled Salamander
____ Mud Salamander
____ Two-toed Amphiuma

**Frogs and Toads**
____ Barking Treefrog
____ Bullfrog
____ Carpenter Frog
____ Cricket Frog
____ Gray Treefrog
____ Fowler's Toad
____ Green Treefrog
____ Leopard Frog
____ Pickerel Frog
____ Southern Toad
____ Spring Peeper

# Fish found in Dismal Swamp and surrounding waterways

____ Longnose Gar
____ Bowfin
____ Redfin Pickerel
____ Chain Pickerel
____ Golden Shiner
____ Blue Catfish
____ White Catfish
____ Channel Catfish
____ Yellow Bullhead
____ Brown Bullhead
____ American Eel
____ Mosquitofish

____ Pirate Perch
____ Mud Sunfish
____ Redbreast Sunfish
____ Pumpkinseed
____ Bluegill
____ Largemouth Bass
____ Black Crappie
____ Striped Bass
____ Eastern Swamp Darter
____ Yellow Perch
____ Eastern Mudminnow
____ Swamp Fish

# References/Resources

Ashley, William E., Jr. 2000. "Early Citizen and Public Support for Preservation of the Dismal Swamp, a Historical Perspective." *The Natural History of the Great Dismal Swamp*, ed. Robert K. Rose, Suffolk, VA: Suffolk-Nansemond Chapter, Izaak Walton League of America, Inc.

Bertie-Camp, Laurie. "Bear That Ruled the Woods Is Part of Hunting Lore." *The Virginian-Pilot*, October 27, 2001.

Bisher, Catherine W. and Southern, Michael T. 1966. *A Guide to the Architecture of Eastern North Carolina*. Chapel Hill, NC: The University of North Carolina Press.

Bishop, Nathaniel H. 1878. *Voyage of the Paper Canoe*. Boston, MA: Lee and Shepherd. Reprint, Wilmington, NC: Coastal Carolina Press, 2000.

Bjorkman, Gwen Boyer. 1990. *Pasquotank County, North Carolina Record of Deeds*. Bowie, MD: Heritage Books, Inc.

Boyd, William K. 1929. *Introduction to the First Edition, History of the Dividing Line*. North Carolina Historical Commission. Republished with a new introduction by Percy G. Adams. New York: Dover Publications, 1969.

Brown, Alexander Crosby. 1981. *Juniper Waterway*. Charlottesville, VA: University of Virginia Press.

Brown, Alexander Crosby. 1970. *The Dismal Swamp Canal*. Chesapeake, VA: Norfolk County Historical Society of Chesapeake.

Campbell, Tom, Personal Communication, December 21, 2001.

Corbett, Roger H. 1977. *Virginia Whitewater*. Springfield, VA: Seneca Press.

Chesapeake Public Utilities. "Dedication of the Northwest River Water Treatment Plant." *Virginian-Pilot Supplement*, June 15, 1999.

City of Chesapeake, VA. www.cityofchesapeake.net. 2001.

Currituck County Bicentennial Committee. 1976. "What's In a Name?" *Currituck County Bicentennial Celebration*.

Currituck County Tricentennial Committee. 1970. "Twenty Ways to Spell Currituck." *Currituck County Tricentennial, 1670-1970*.

Daniel, Mac. "Refuge Borders Closing in on Black Bears." *Virginian Pilot*, May 10, 1994.

Daniel, Mac. "Chesapeake Span is New Bridge to Old Times." *Virginian Pilot*. September 8, 1996.

Duke, Alvah. 1975. *Bicentennial Map of the Great Dismal Swamp*. Chesapeake, VA.

Emmerson, John C. Jr. "Steam Navigation in Virginia and Northeastern North Carolina Waters, 1826-1836." *Norfolk and Portsmouth Herald*.

Fischer, David Hackett and Kelly, James C. 2000. *Bound Away, Virginia and the Westward Movement*. Charlottesville, VA: The University Press of Virginia.

Floyd, Larry. Personal Communication, December, 2003.

Forehand, W.W. 1977. "From the Past to the Present." *Historical Highlights of Camden County 1777 - 1977*. Elizabeth City, NC: Carolina Printing Company.

Gammon, Pat. Personal Communication, November 9, 2002.

Hanbury, Elizabeth Baum. 1985. *Currituck Legacy, The Baum Family of North Carolina*. Chesapeake, VA.

Hathaway, J.R.R. October 1900. *Records of Albemarle County*. Edenton, NC: The North Carolina Historical and Genealogical Register. Reprinted, Baltimore: Genealogical Publishing Company, Inc., 1979.

Henderson, Archibald. *North Carolina, The Old North State and the New*. Vol. 2, 1941. Chicago: The Lewis Publishing Company.

The Historical Committee. 1970. *Currituck County Tricentennial Celebration, Report of the Historical Committee on Outstanding Citizens, 1670-1970*. Currituck County, NC: The Currituck Historical Society.

Hudgins, Dennis Ray. 1999. *Cavaliers and Pioneers, Abstracts of Virginia Land Patents and Grants*. Vol. 7, 1762-1776. Richmond, VA: Virginia Genealogical Society.

Jones, Thalia T. 1977. "Transportation in Colonial Days." *Historical Highlights of Camden County, 1777-1977*. Camden County Historical Society, Elizabeth City, NC: Carolina Printing Company.

Kaufman, Wallace and Pilkey, Orrin. 1979. *The Beaches Are Moving*. Garden City, NY: Anchor Press/Doubleday.

La Vere, David. "Shipping Lanes," *Our State, Down Home in North Carolina*, May, 2003. Greensboro, NC: Mann Media.

Leary-Smith, Penny. Personal Communication, April 27, 2001.

Levy, Gerald. "The Great Dismal Swamp: Folklore and Poem," "History of the Swamp: The Story," "History of the Swamp: The Setting," "History of the Swamp: The Creatures," (lectures, Old Dominion University Elderhostel, Portsmouth, VA).

Lundgren, Kevin. Personal Communication, July 2, 2001.

Mather, Mike. "Young Bear Turns Up As Beach Tourist," *Virginian-Pilot*, May 26, 1994.

McKnight, Floyd. 1959. "The Great Dismal Swamp." *History of Lower Tidewater Virginia*, ed. Rogers Dey Whichard. New York, NY: Lewis Historical Publishing Company, Inc.

Monzingo, Shirley. "Former Air Station Evolves into Secluded Subdivision." *Virginian Pilot*, December 16, 2000.

Morris, Rhonda. Personal Communication, Oct. 9, 2002.

National Register of Historic Places. www.hpo.dcr.state.nc.us/nrlist.htm, 2001.

The Nature Conservancy. "Andy Griffith Donates Wetlands." *Virginia Chapter News*, Fall/Winter, 1998.

North Carolina Atlas and Gazetteer. Freeport, Maine: DeLorme Mapping. 1993.

Nugent, Nell Marion. 1992. *Cavaliers and Pioneers, Abstracts of Virginia Land Patents and Grants*, Vol. 1, 1623-1666. Richmond, VA: Virginia State Library.

Nugent, Nell Marion. 1977. *Cavaliers and Pioneers, Abstracts of Virginia Land Patents and Grants*, Volume 2, 1666-1695. Richmond, VA: Virginia State Library.

Nugent, Nell Marion. 1992. *Cavaliers and Pioneers, Abstracts of Virginia Land Patents and Grants*, Volume 3, 1695-1732. Richmond, VA: Virginia State Library.

Pendergraft, Don. "The Air Up There: The United States Naval Station at Weeksville," Spring, 2001. Tar Heel Junior Historian.

Pugh, Jesse Forbes. 1953. *Journeys Through Camden County*. Elizabeth City, NC: Pasquotank County Library.

Pugh, Jesse Forbes. 1957. *300 Years Along the Pasquotank, A Biographical History of Camden County*. Durham, NC: Seeman Printery, Inc.

Pugh, Jesse Forbes. 1973. "A Study of John Gibbs." *The Journal of the Currituck Historical Society*. Vol. 1(2). Currituck County Historical Society.

Pugh, Jesse F. and Williams, Frank T. 1964. *The Hotel in the Dismal Swamp*. Richmond, VA: Garrett and Massie, Inc.

Ramsey, George. 2000. *Stone Mileposts Along the Dismal Swamp Canal*. Virginia Beach, VA: Carnette Printing.

Ramsey, George. Conversations, January 22, 2001, July 10, 2001, December, 2003.

Rankin, Hugh F. 1962. *Upheaval in Albemarle: The Story of Culpeper's Rebellion*. Raleigh, NC: The Carolina Charter Tercentenary Commission.

Rights, Douglas. 1957. "Pasquotankís Indians." *Year Book*. Elizabeth City, NC: Pasquotank Historical Society.

Ruffin, Edmund. 1861. *Agricultural, Geological and Descriptive Sketches of Lower North Carolina*. Raleigh, NC.

Simpson, Bland. 1990. *The Great Dismal*. Chapel Hill, NC: The University of North Carolina Press.

Snell, Tee Loftin. 1974. *The Wild Shores, America's Beginnings*. Washington, DC: National Geographic Society.

Stevens, Howard J. 1999. *Albemarle People and Places*. Elizabeth City, NC: Family Research Society of Northeastern North Carolina, Inc.

Tennant, Diane. "Swept Away, Shifting Sands Cover What Once Was Seagull, N.C." *Virginian Pilot*, December 2, 2001.

Terwilliger, Karen. 2000, "Breeding Birds in Two Atlantic White Cedar Stands in the Great Dismal Swamp." *The Natural History of the Great Dismal Swamp*, ed. Robert K. Rose. Suffolk, VA: Suffolk-Nansemond Chapter, Izaak Walton League of America, Inc.

Trout, W.E. 1998. *The Great Dismal Atlas*. Palmyra, VA: Palmyra Press.

U.S. Fish and Wildlife Service. January 2004. *The Great Dismal Swamp and the Underground Railroad*. http://www.fws.gov.

Wallace, Elizabeth Curtis. Edited by Cross, Eleanor P. and Charles B., Jr. 1983. *Glencoe Diary, The War-Time Journal of Elizabeth Curtis Wallace*. Chesapeake, VA: Norfolk County Historical Society of Chesapeake, Virginia.

Welsh, Marion Fiske. 1982. *Moyock, A Pictorial and Folk History 1900-1920*. Norfolk, VA: The Donning Company/Publishers, Inc.

Whichard, Rogers Dey. 1959. *The History of Lower Tidewater Virginia*. New York, NY: Lewis Historical Publishing Company, Inc.

Wood, John Elliott. 1974. "Report of the Committee on Historic Sites, 2 January, 1957," *The Journal of the Currituck Historical Society*, Vol. 1, No. 2.

## Organizations

**Albemarle Resource Conservation and Development Council**
730 Granville Street
Edenton, NC 27932

**Currituck County Tourism Development Authority**
PO Box 1160
Grandy, NC 27939
www.currituckchamber.org

**Dismal Swamp Canal Visitor Center**
2356 US Hwy 17 N
South Mills, VA 27976
www.DismalSwamp.com

**Elizabeth City Chamber of Commerce**
PO Box 426
Elizabeth City, NC 27907
(252) 335-4365
www.elizabethcity.chamber.org

**Izaak Walton League of America**
707 Conservation Lane
Gaithersburg, MD 20878
(800) 453-5463
www.iwla.org

**North Carolina's Northeast**
119 Water St.
Edenton, NC 27932
(888) 872-8562
www.ncnortheast.com

**Preservation North Carolina Northeast Regional Office**
420 Elliott Street
Edenton, NC 27932
(252) 482-7455

**The Nature Conservancy Green Sea Program**
940-B Corporate Lane
Chesapeake, VA 23320
(757) 549-4690

**The Virginia Canals and Navigations Society**
6826 Rosemont Drive
McLean, VA 22101

## Federal Agencies

**Great Dismal Swamp National Wildlife Refuge**
3100 Desert Road
Suffolk, VA 23434
(757) 986-3705
http://greatdismalswamp.fws.gov

**U.S. Fish and Wildlife Service**
Southeast Region
1875 Century Center Blvd NE
Atlanta, GA 30345
(404) 679-7082

**U.S. Army Corps of Engineers**
Norfolk District
803 Front Street
Norfolk, VA 23510
(757) 441-7652

## *State Agencies*

**Department of Conservation and Recreation**
217 Governor Street, 3rd Floor
Richmond, VA 23210
(804) 786-7951
www.state.va.us/~dcr/vaher.html

**North Carolina Department of Agriculture & Consumer Services**
PO Box 27647
Raleigh, NC 27611
(919) 733-2290
www.ncagr.com

**North Carolina Department of Cultural Resources**
4604 MSC
Raleigh, NC 27699
(919) 733-1620
www.ncdcr.org

**North Carolina Department of Transportation**
1503 MSC
Raleigh, NC 27699
(919) 733-2522
www.dot.state.nc.us

**North Carolina Department of Transportation, Ferry Division**
113 Arendell St., Room 120
Morehead City, NC 28557
(800) 293-3779

**North Carolina Division of Forest Resources**
1616 MSC
Raleigh, NC 27699
(919) 733-2162
www.dfr.state.nc.us

**North Carolina Division of Marine Fisheries**
113 Arendell St.
Morehead City, NC 28557
(800) 682-32632
www.ncfisheries.net

**North Carolina Division of Parks and Recreation Department of Environment and Natural Resources**
P.O. Box 27687
Raleigh, NC 27611
(919) 733-PARK

**North Carolina Division of Parks and Recreation**
1615 MSC
Raleigh, NC 27699
(919) 733-4181
www.ncparks.net

**North Carolina Historic Sites**
4620 MSC
Raleigh, NC 27699
(919) 733-9515
www.ah.dcr.state.nc.us/section/hs

**North Carolina Horse Council**
PO Box 12999
Raleigh, NC 27605
(919) 821-11030
www.nchorsecouncil.com

**North Carolina Visitor Information Center/Dismal Swamp Canal**
2356 US Hwy 17 N.
South Mills, VA 27976
(252) 771-8333
www.icw-net.com/dscwelcome

North Carolina Wildlife Resources Commission
512 N. Salisbury St.
Raleigh, NC 27604
(919) 733-7083
www.ncwildlife.org

Virginia Department of Game and Inland Fisheries
PO Box 11104
Richmond, VA 23230
www.dgif.state.va.us

## County Agencies

Currituck County Tourism Development Authority
PO Box 1160
Grandy, NC 27939
www.currituckchamber.org

## City Agencies

City of Chesapeake Parks and Recreation Department
112 Mann Drive
Chesapeake, VA 23320
(757) 382-6411

City of Suffolk
Department of Parks and Recreation
301 N. Main St.
Suffolk, VA 23434
(757) 923-2360

City of Suffolk Division of Tourism
321 North Main Street
Suffolk, VA 23434
(757) 923-3880

Elizabeth City Area Chamber of Commerce
McMorrine and Ehringhaus Streets
P. O. Box 426
Elizabeth City, NC 27907
(252) 335-4365
www.elizcity.com

Knobb's Creek Recreation Center
East Ward Street
Elizabeth City, NC 27909
(252) 335-1424

Northwest River Park
1733 Indian Creek Road
Chesapeake, VA 23322
(757) 421-3145 or 421-7151
www.cityofchesapeake.net

## Genealogy Resources

Family Research Society of Northeastern North Carolina, Inc.
P.O. Box 1425
Elizabeth City, NC 27906
(252) 333-1640

Virginia Genealogical Society
5001 West Broad Street #115
Richmond, VA 23230
(804) 285-8954
www.vgs.org/

Virginia Historical Society
428 North Boulevard
Richmond, VA 23221
(804) 358-4901
www.vahistorical.org

Library of Virginia/Archives Research
800 East Broad Street
Richmond, VA 23219
(804) 692-3888
www.lva.lib.va.us/pubserv/genie.htm

## General Information

Albemarle Resource Conservation and Development Council
Edenton, NC 27932
(252) 482-7437

American Canoe Association
7432 Alban Station Blvd, Suite B-232
Springfield, VA 22150
(703) 451-0141; www.acanet.org

North Carolina Association of
Convention &Visitors Bureaus
1235E East Blvd. #213
Charlotte, NC 28203
(704) 333-8455; www.visitnc.org

North Carolina Association of
Festivals & Events
PO Box 1642
Lexington, NC 27293
(800) 555-2142, PIN # 6188
www.ncfestivals.com

North Carolina Association of
RV Parks & Campgrounds
893 US Hwy 70W, Suite 202
Garner, NC 27529
(919) 779-5709; www.ncarvc.com

North Carolina Bed &
Breakfasts & Inns
PO Box 1029
Carolina Beach, NC 28428
(800) 849-5392; www.ncbbi.org

North Carolina Hotel &
Motel Association
PO Box 30457
Raleigh, NC 27622
(919) 786-9730; www.visitnc.org

North Carolina Professional
Paddlesports Association
PO Box 145
Rosman, NC 28772
(828) 877-3557
www.paddlenorthcarolina.org

Virginia Professional Paddlesports
Association
7432 Alban Station Blvd
Suite A-111
Springfield, VA 22150
(703) 451-3864; www.propaddle.com

USA Canoe and Kayak
PO Box 789
Lake Placid, NY 12946
(513) 523-1855; www.usack.org

# Web Sites

The Bonny Blue - tours on the
Dismal Swamp Canal
www.bonnyblue.com

Chesapeake, Virginia
www.chesapeake.com

"Chessie Watch Page"
www.sirenian.org/chessie.html

City of Chesapeake
www.chesapeake.va.us

City of Suffolk
www.suffolk.va.us

Coastal Waters Heritage Tourism
www.ncwaterways.com

Currituck Beach Lighthouse
www.curritucklight.com

Currituck County Chamber
of Commerce
www.currituckchamber.com

Currituck County Government
www.co.currituck.nc.us

Currituck/Knotts Island Ferry
www.ncferry.org

Dismal Swamp Canal Visitor
Information Center
www.icw.net/dscwelcome

Genealogy
www.genealogy.com

Great Dismal Swamp National
Wildlife Refuge
http://greatdismalswamp.fws.gov

The Great Dismal Swamp and the
Underground Railroad
http://www.fws.gov.

Historic Albemarle Tour
www.albemarle-nc.com/hat

**Merchant's Millpond State Park**
www.albemarle-nc.com
/gates/millpond.htmll

**Mountains to Sea Trail**
www.ncmst.org

**North Carolina Archaeology**
www.arch.dcr.state.nc.us

**North Carolina Coastal Paddle Trails**
http://www.ncsu.edu/paddle
trails/albemarle

**North Carolina Coastal Plain Paddle Trails Guide**
http://ils.unc.edu/parkproject/nc
trails.html

**North Carolina Department of Transportation, Ferry Division**
www.ncferry.org

**North Carolina Division of Tourism, Film and Sports Development**
Department of Commerce
www.vistnc.com

**Outer Banks Tourism**
www.outerbanksbeachguide.com

**Save Our Light**
www.saveourlight.com

**United States Army Corps of Engineers**
www.usace.army.mil

**United States Coast Guard Office of Boating Safety**
www.uscgboating.org

**Virginia Birding and Wildlife Trail**
www.dgif.state.va.us

**Virginia Native Plant Society**
www.hort.vt.edu/VNPS

# Index

# Other Eco Images Titles
## of Related Interest

### Bayside History Trail
*A View From the Water*
by Lillie Gilbert, Belinda Nash & Deni Norred-Williams
ISBN: 0-938423-09-6

### A Trek to the Top of Mount Kilimanjaro
*Africa's Highest Mountain*
by Ann Brand, Ed. D.
ISBN: 0-938423-10-X

### Listening With The Soles of My Feet
by Rosemary Chute
ISBN: 0-938423-05-3

If you would like to receive a free catalog featuring additional
Eco Images books, please contact:

**Eco Images**
P.O. Box 61413
Virginia Beach, VA  23466-1413

(757) 421-3929  •  wildfood@infionline.net
www.wildfood.home.infionline.net